The Metropolitan Opera Presents

Pietro Mascagni's
Cavalleria Rusticana

Ruggero Leoncavallo's
Pagliacci

Metropolitan Opera House,
ABBEY, SCHOEFFEL & GRAU, *Sole Lessees and Managers.*

GRAND OPERA
UNDER THE DIRECTION OF

HENRY E. ABBEY AND MAURICE GRAU.

Friday Evening, Dec. 22d,
at 8:15 o'clock,

LEONCAVALLO'S OPERA,

PAGLIACCI,

NEDDA...................................Mme. MELBA
AND
TONIO.................................Sig. ANCONA
SILVIO...............................Sig. GROMZESKI
PEPPE.................................Sig. GUETARY
AND
CANIO................................Sig. DE LUCIA
CONDUCTOR, . . Sig. MANCINELLI.

FOLLOWED BY MASCAGNI'S OPERA,

Cavalleria Rusticana.

SANTUZZA.............................Madame CALVE
LUCIA...............................Mlle. BAUERMEISTER
AND
LOLA................................Mlle. GUERCIA
ALFIO................................M. MARTAPOURA
AND
TURIDDU . ...Sig. VIGNAS
CONDUCTOR, . . Sig. BEVIGNANI.

REGISSEUR..............................Mons. CASTELMARY
STAGE MANAGER..........................Mr. WILLIAM PARRY

The Knabe Pianos used at the Metropolitan Opera House and
by the Artists of the Company.

Mason & Hamlin Liszt Organ used.

On December 22, 1893, the Met presented the first-ever
performance of *Pagliacci* and *Cavalleria Rusticana* as a double bill

The Metropolitan Opera Presents

Pietro Mascagni's
Cavalleria Rusticana

Music by Pietro Mascagni

Libretto by Giovanni Targioni-Tozzetti and Guido Menasci

Based on a play and short story by Giovanni Verga

Ruggero Leoncavallo's
Pagliacci

Music and libretto by Ruggero Leoncavallo

AMADEUS
PRESS
An Imprint of Hal Leonard Corporation

The Met
ropolitan
Opera

Published in 2015 by Amadeus Press
An Imprint of Hal Leonard Corporation
7777 West Bluemound Road
Milwaukee, WI 53213

Trade Book Division Editorial Offices
33 Plymouth St., Montclair, NJ 07042

English translations of libretti copyright © 2000 by Leyerle Publications, 28 Stanley Street, Mt. Morris, New York 14510. English translations by Nico Castel. Originally published by Leyerle Publications as part of *Verismo Opera Libretti*. These publications, and others in the Leyerle Opera Libretti series, are available directly from Leyerle's website at www.leyerlepublications.com.

Printed in the United States of America

Book design by Mark Lerner
Library of Congress Cataloging-in-Publication Data is available upon request.

ISBN 978-1-57467-463-7

www.amadeuspress.com

CONTENTS

Enrico Caruso (Turiddu), conductor Arturo Toscanini, and Emmy Destinn (Santuzza), seated from left, with the cast of the 1908 production of *Cavalleria Rusticana*
METROPOLITAN OPERA ARCHIVES

INTRODUCTION

On December 22, 1893, the youthful Metropolitan Opera company—then in its tenth season—presented a double bill of two one-act operas that had recently premiered in Italy. It was the first time these two works had ever been performed back to back, and, as the *New York Times* laconically declared, "The effect of bringing the two operas together in one night was good." Audiences agreed, and since that day, *Cavalleria Rusticana* and *Pagliacci* have become inseparable on stages all over the world, their pairing affectionately known as *Cav/Pag*. The melodies Mascagni and Leoncavallo created—most notably *Cavalleria*'s orchestral intermezzo and Canio's aria that ends Act I of *Pagliacci*—have long taken on a life of their own outside the world of opera. But it's only as part of the scores they were written for that these pieces reveal their full dramatic potential.

Like the previous volumes of the Metropolitan Opera Presents series, this book is designed to give you an in-depth introduction to two of opera's most enduringly popular works. In addition to the complete libretti in Italian and English, you will find synopses, a detailed program note with historical background, and the "In Focus" feature we provide in the Met's house program every night—a brief summary of key aspects of the operas. We've also included many archival photos of some of the greatest stars who have appeared at the Met in 120 years of *Cav/Pag* performances.

Whether you watch these operas in the theater, as part of our *Live in HD* movie-theater transmissions, or experience them as a radio broadcast or web stream, we hope this book will give you all the information you need to enjoy two of opera's most beloved works.

To learn more about Met productions, Live in HD *movie-theater transmissions, Met membership, and more, visit metopera.org.*

The Metropolitan Opera Presents

Pietro Mascagni's
Cavalleria Rusticana

Ruggero Leoncavallo's
Pagliacci

Pietro Mascagni's
Cavalleria Rusticana

Emma Calvé as Santuzza, 1893
FALK / METROPOLITAN OPERA ARCHIVES

Synopsis

A village in Sicily. At dawn on Easter Sunday, Turiddu is heard in the distance singing of his love for Lola, wife of the carter Alfio. She and Turiddu had been a couple before he went to join the army. When he returned and found her married to Alfio, he took up with Santuzza and seduced her, but now has abandoned her and rekindled his relationship with Lola. Later in the morning, a distraught Santuzza approaches the tavern of Mamma Lucia, Turiddu's mother, who tells her that her son is away buying wine. But Santuzza knows that Turiddu has been seen during the night in the village. Alfio arrives with a group of men, boasting of his horses—and of Lola. He asks Mamma Lucia if she has any more of her good wine. When she says that Turiddu has gone to get more, Alfio replies that he saw the other man near his house that same morning. Lucia is surprised, but Santuzza tells her to keep quiet. As the villagers follow the procession to church, Santuzza stays behind and pours out her grief about Turiddu to Mamma Lucia. The old woman expresses her pity, then also leaves for mass. Turiddu appears and is confronted by Santuzza about his affair with Lola but denies her accusations. Just then Lola passes by on her way to church. She mocks Santuzza, and Turiddu turns to follow her, but Santuzza begs him to stay and implores him not to abandon her. Turiddu refuses to listen and leaves, cursed by Santuzza. Alfio arrives, late for mass. Santuzza tells him that Lola went to church with Turiddu and reveals that his wife has been cheating on him. In a rage, Alfio swears to get even and rushes off, leaving behind the now conscience-stricken Santuzza.

Returning from the church, the villagers gather at Mamma Lucia's tavern. Turiddu leads them in a drinking song, but the atmosphere becomes tense when Alfio appears. He refuses Turiddu's offer of wine and instead challenges him to a knife fight. Turiddu admits his guilt but is determined to go through with the fight, for Santuzza's sake as well as for his honor. The two men agree to meet outside the village. Alone with his mother, Turiddu begs her to take care of Santuzza if he doesn't come back, then runs off to the fight. As Mamma Lucia waits anxiously, shouts are heard in the distance. A woman runs in screaming that Turiddu has been killed.

In Focus

William Berger

Premiere: Teatro Costanzi, Rome
May 17, 1890

Cavalleria Rusticana is a story of passion and jealousy in a rough Sicilian village, told with the force of primal myth. The opera is based on the highly influential short story of the same name by Sicilian writer Giovanni Verga, which created a sensation with its straightforward yet evocative prose that was so radically different from the flowery, dense style that had been common in Italian literature. Mascagni created a musical counterpart to Verga's achievement—his score seems to be a direct expression of the characters' emotions without any comment or adornment on the part of its author. *Cavalleria* won first prize in a competition for one-act operas by emerging composers (Puccini was another contestant) and took the operatic world by storm at its premiere. It earned delirious praise and equally vehement antipathy and has never been out of the core repertory. Its success was crucial in launching the verismo movement in opera, inspiring other composers to turn to stories and characters from real life (and often from society's grungier elements). The influence of verismo reached well beyond the dozen operas that can safely be categorized as the core of the genre (perhaps most famously Puccini's *La Bohème* and Leoncavallo's

Pagliacci). It is a strain that has also run through the neo-realist Italian cinematic masterpieces of the mid-20th century, and more recently can be seen in the films of such directors as Lars von Trier. *Cavalleria Rusticana*, then, is among the most influential operas and one of the most important in terms of defining the art form as a whole. But beyond any historical considerations, it remains a vital music drama as gripping in many ways as it was at its first performance. The intense characterizations and the plot with its sense of moving toward a cataclysmic ending, all of it deftly woven into an evocative setting, make it one of the most relentlessly exciting works in the repertory.

The Creators

Pietro Mascagni (1863–1945) studied at the Milan Conservatory with Amilcare Ponchielli and even shared a small apartment for a while with fellow student Giacomo Puccini. *Cavalleria Rusticana* made Mascagni rich and famous literally overnight, and although he was not the one-hit wonder he has been labeled by non-Italian critics, his long, varied, and controversial career never quite hit the same apex again. The then-unknown librettists Giovanni Targioni-Tozzetti and Guido Menasci earned praise for their excellent work on *Cavalleria Rusticana* and went on to provide other libretti for Mascagni, Leoncavallo, and other composers of the day. Author Giovanni Verga (1840–1922) was born in Catania, Sicily, and used the imagery of his native land in his novels and stories. Among these, *Cavalleria Rusticana* was perhaps the most celebrated, packing a wallop in a mere four pages of razor-sharp prose. Verga adapted the story into a play, featuring the legendary actress Eleonora Duse, that achieved great fame and notoriety in Italy.

The Setting

The setting of *Cavalleria Rusticana* in the piazza of a Sicilian village in the 1880s is not merely picturesque. The village is, in a sense, a character in the opera, and is key to its dramatic and musical weight. The place is crude, untouched by modernity, close to nature's cycles of life and death and the primitive human rituals associated with them. It's dirt-poor but stabilized by codes of conduct and mores so ancient that no one remembers—or questions—their original intent. The drama unfolds on Easter Sunday. David McVicar's new Met production sets the action around 1900, a few years after the opera's composition.

The Music

The score of *Cavalleria* is direct, unadorned, and honest. Early critics who complained of its crassness and lack of artistry were paying it an unwitting compliment. The famous intermezzo, often heard outside the context of the opera, summarizes its musical plan: gorgeous, melancholy melody carried by unison strings with very little harmonization. The opera opens with the tenor's traditional Sicilian song, performed from a distance and flowing across the empty stage, suggesting a deep connection between characters and their environment. This was a startling effect in 1890 (and the same idea appeared hardly less startling 50 years later in the musical *Oklahoma!*). The impassioned vocal solos in *Cavalleria Rusticana* used to be sung with a considerable amount of extra-musical effects, such as sobs, gasps, and shouted words, especially in Italy. This delivery is less in style now. Some artists have pointed out that the secret is to make the audience believe a word has been screamed when it was, in fact, sung. Santuzza, the leading female role, is sung by both sopranos and mezzo-sopranos; her great aria, "Voi lo sapete," is a stirring challenge to the singer's musical and dramatic abilities, and her solo voice leads the impressive Easter chorus. The tenor's equally impassioned farewell, "Mamma, quel vino è generoso," amounts to a suicide aria as all-encompassing as any in opera, while his confrontational duet with Santuzza becomes a clash of archetypes.

Cavalleria Rusticana and *Pagliacci* at the Met

Cavalleria was first performed by the Met on tour in Chicago in December 1891, paired with Act I of Verdi's *La Traviata*. *Pagliacci* followed in December 1893 at the opera house in New York, in a double bill with Gluck's *Orfeo ed Euridice*. The Met was the first opera company to present *Cav/Pag* together on December 22, 1893 (with *Pagliacci* performed first), but occasional pairings with other operas were still common into the early 20th century. *Cavalleria* and *Pagliacci* individually shared the Met stage with such diverse works as *Il Barbiere di Siviglia*, *Don Pasquale*, *Lucia di Lammermoor*, *La Fille du Régiment*, *Il Trovatore*, *Rigoletto*, *La Bohème*, and even Rimsky-Korsakov's *Le Coq d'Or*. An unlikely double bill of *Pagliacci* and *Hansel and Gretel* was especially popular, with almost 100 performances between 1906 and 1938. Among the notable early interpreters of the leading roles were Emma Eames, Emma Calvé, Johanna Gadski, Olive Fremstad, Emmy Destinn, and Rosa Ponselle (Santuzza); Francesco Tamagno and Enrico Caruso (Turiddu); Nellie Melba, Destinn, Lucrezia Bori, Claudia Muzio, and Queena Mario (Nedda); Caruso (more than 100 performances) and Giovanni Martinelli (Canio); and Pasquale Amato (Tonio). A new production in 1951 starred Zinka Milanov and Richard Tucker in *Cavalleria* and Delia Rigal, Ramón Vinay, and Leonard Warren in *Pagliacci*. This was succeeded by another new staging in 1958, with Lucine Amara as Nedda, Mario Del Monaco as Canio, and Milanov and Warren reprising their roles. The following production, directed and designed by Franco Zeffirelli, premiered in 1970 with Leonard Bernstein conducting a cast that included Grace Bumbry and Franco Corelli in *Cavalleria* and Amara, Richard Tucker, and Sherrill Milnes in *Pagliacci*. Among the many other artists who have appeared in the two operas since the late 1950s are Giulietta Simionato, Eileen Farrell, Fiorenza Cossotto, and Tatiana Troyanos (Santuzza); Teresa Stratas and Diana Soviero (Nedda); Jon Vickers, James McCracken, and Giuseppe Giacomini (Canio); and Cornell

MacNeil and Juan Pons (Tonio). Tenors who have faced the challenge of taking on both leading roles in the same performance include Plácido Domingo, Roberto Alagna, and José Cura. The Met's latest new production, directed by David McVicar, opens in April 2015 with Eva-Maria Westbroek as Santuzza, Patricia Racette as Nedda, and Marcelo Álvarez singing Turiddu and Canio.

CAVALLERIA RUSTICANA

(Rustic Chivalry)

PERSONNAGES

Turiddu, un giovane contadino: tenore
Alfio, un carrettiere: baritono
Santuzza, una giovane Contadina: soprano
Lucia, sua madre: soprano
Lola, sua moglie: mezzosoprano

CHARACTERS

Turiddu, a young soldier: tenor
Alfio, the village drover: baritone
Santuzza, a village girl: soprano
Mamma Lucia, owner of the local tavern and Turiddu's mother: mezzo-soprano
Lola, Alfio's wife: mezzo-soprano

La scena rappresenta una piazza in un paese della Sicilia.
The action takes place in a Sicilian village, on Easter Day in the 1890s.

TURIDDU
(a sipario calato)
(offstage)[1]
O Lola ch'ai di latti la cammisa,[2]
O Lola, who have of milk the blouse,
(Oh Lola of the white blouse,)

e bianca e russa comu la cirasa,
and white and red as the cherry,
(white-skinned and cherry-red lips,)

quannu t'affacci fai la vucca a risa,
whenever you show yourself you make your mouth to smile,
(whenever you appear at the window you smile,)

biato cui ti dà lu primu vasu!
fortunate who gives you the first kiss!
(fortunate is he who gives you the first kiss!)

Ntra la porta tua lu sangu è sparsu
Inside the door yours the blood is spilled

e num me mporta si ce muoru accisu.
and I don't care if there I die murdered.

E s'iddu muoru e vaju mparadisu,
And if I die and go to paradise,

si nun ce truovo a ttia, mancu ce trasu!
if I don't find you I won't stay!

(Nel fondo, a destra, c'è una chiesa con porta praticabile. A sinistra l'osteria e la casa di Mamma Lucia. È il giorno di Pasqua.)

(The curtain is raised. It is Easter morning and the square is deserted. One sees the facade of a church to one side and Mamma Lucia's tavern to the other. The voices of the villagers can be heard from afar.)

DONNE VOCI
WOMEN'S VOICES
(di dentro)
(inside)
Gli aranci olezzano sui verdi margini,
The orange trees perfume the green verges,

cantan le allodole tra i mirti in fior;
sing the larks amid the myrtles in flower;

tempo è si mormori da ognuno il tenero canto
it is time to murmur by each one the tender song

che i palpiti raddoppia al cor.
that the beating redoubles of the heart.
(it is time to sing the tender song that quickens the beating of the heart.)

(Le donne entrano in scena.)
(The women come on stage.)

VOCI UOMO
MEN'S VOICES
In mezzo al campo tra le spiche d'oro
Amid the field among the ears of corn golden

giunge il rumore delle vostre spole,
arrives the noise of your shuttles,[3]

noi stanchi, riposando dal lavoro,

we, tired, resting from our labors,

a voi pensiamo, o belle occhi di sole
of you are thinking, oh beautiful eyes-of-sun
(we think of you, our bright-eyed pretty ones)

a voi corriamo, come vola l'augello al suo richiamo.
to you we run, as flies the bird to its mating call.

(Gli uomini entrano in scena.)
(The men come on stage.)

DONNE
WOMEN
Cessin le rustiche opre;
Cease the rural labors;

la Vergine serena allietasi del Salvator.
the Virgin serene rejoices in the Savior.

Tempo è si mormori da ognuno il tenero canto che i palpiti rad-doppia al cor.

(Gli uomini e le donne a poco a poco si spengono, come Santuzza entra e si avvicina Mamma Lucia, in piedi davanti alla sua taverna agitato.)
(The men and women gradually go off, as Santuzza agitatedly enters and approaches Mamma Lucia, standing outside her tavern.)

SANTUZZA[4]
Dite, Mamma Lucia . . .
Tell me, Mamma Lucia . . .

MAMMA LUCIA
(sorpresa)
(surprised to see her)
Sei tu? . . . Che vuoi?
It's you? . . . What do you want?

SANTUZZA
Turiddu[5] ov'è?
Turiddu, where is he?

LUCIA
Fin qui vieni a cercare il figlio mio?
Even here you come to look for the son mine?

SANTUZZA
Voglio saper soltanto, perdonatemi voi, dove trovarlo.
I want to know merely, forgive me, where to find him.

LUCIA
Non lo so; non voglio brighe!
I don't know; I don't want trouble!

SANTUZZA
Mamma Lucia, vi supplico piangendo,
Mamma Lucia, I beg you, in tears,

fate come il Signore a Maddalena,
do as did the Lord to (Mary) Magdalen,

ditemi per pietà dov'è Turiddu?
tell me, for pity's sake, where is Turiddu?

LUCIA
È andato per il vino a Francofonte.

He's gone for wine in Francofonte.

SANTUZZA
No! L'han visto in paese ad alta notte.
No! They saw him in the village late at night.

LUCIA
Che dici? Se non è tornato a casa! Entra!
What are you saying? (But) he hasn't been home! Come inside!

SANTUZZA
Non posso entrare in casa vostra . . . Sono scomunicata! . . .
I cannot enter into your house . . . I am excommunicated! . . . [6]

LUCIA
E che ne sai del mio figliolo?
And what do you know about my son?

SANTUZZA
Quale spina ho in core!
What a thorn I have in my heart!

(S'ode il rumore degli zoccoli di cavallo, dei sonagli e della frusta.
Entra Alfio su un carrettino, accompagnato da alcuni uomini.)
(The sound of horses' hooves, the jingling of harness bells, and the cracking
of a whip are heard. Alfio enters on his cart accompanied by some men.)

ALFIO
Il cavallo scalpita, i sonagli squillano,
The horse paws the ground, the harness bells jingle,

schiocca la frusta. Ehi là!
crack the whip. Hey there!

Soffi il vento gelido, cada l'acqua o nevichi,
Let blow the wind icy, let fall the water or let it snow,

a me che cosa fa?
to me what does it matter?

UOMINI
MEN
Oh che bel mestiere fare il carrettiere,
Oh what a jolly occupation to be a carter,

andar di qua e di là!
to go from here and there!

ALFIO
Schiocchi la frusta!

M'aspetta a casa Lola, che m'ama e mi consola,[7]
She awaits me at home Lola, who loves me and consoles me,

ch'è tutta fedeltà.
who is all loyalty.
(Lola who loves and consoles me awaits me at home, loyalty itself.)

Il cavallo scalpiti,[8] **i sonagli squillino,**
The horse, let it paw the ground, the harness bells let them jingle,

è Pasqua ed io son qua!
it's Easter and I am here!

LUCIA
(di Alfio)
(to Alfio)
Beato voi, compar Alfio, che siete sempre allegro così!

How lucky you, neighbor Alfio, who are always happy like that!

ALFIO
Mamma Lucia, n'avete ancora di quel vecchio vino?
Mamma Lucia, have you still of that old wine?
                    (do you still have some of that old wine of yours?)

LUCIA
Non so; Turiddu è andato a provvederne.
I don't know. Turiddu has gone to get some.

ALFIO
S'è sempre qui! L'ho visto stamattina vicino a casa mia.
But he is always here! I saw him this morning near my house.

LUCIA
Come?
What?

SANTUZZA
(a parte, a Lucia, in una voce tace)
(aside, to Lucia, in a hushed voice)
Tacete!
Hush!

ALFIO
Io me ne vado, ite voi altrie in chiesa.
I am leaving, go you all to church.
                    (you two go to church.)

(Esce.)
(He leaves.)

CORO
CHORUS
(Latin) *Regina coeli laetare. Alleluja!*
Queen of heaven rejoice. Alleluiah!

Quia quem meruisti portare, resurrenxit sicut dixit.
She who Him was worthy to bear, risen from the dead as prophesied.

(Gruppi di persone vanno ad inginocchiarsi davanti alla chiesa.)
(A group of people appear and kneel before the church.)

CORO
CHORUS
Inneggiamo, il Signor non è morto!
Let us sing hymns, the Lord is not dead!

Ei fulgente ha dischiuso l'avel.
He, radiant, has opened the tomb.

Inneggiamo al Signore risorto,
Let us sing hymns to the Lord risen,

oggi asceso alla gloria del ciel.
today ascended to the glory of heaven.

CORO
CHORUS
(dall'interno della chiesa)
(from inside the church)
Alleluja!

SANTUZZA
Inneggiamo, il Signor non è morto, Inneggiamo al Signore risorto,
etc.

(Tutti entrano in chiesa tranne Santuzza e Lucia.)
(At the end of this chorus all enter the church except Santuzza and Mamma Lucia.)

LUCIA
(a Santuzza)
(to Santuzza)
Perché m'hai fatto segno di tacere?
Why did you to me make sign to keep quiet?
(Why did you tell me before to keep quiet?)

SANTUZZA
Voi lo sapete, o mamma, prima d'andar soldato
You know it, oh mamma, before going off solider
                              (before he went into the army)

Turiddu aveva a Lola eterna fè giurato.
Turiddu had to Lola eternal faith sworn.
(Turiddu swore to Lola a vow of eternal faith.)

Tornò, la seppe sposa; e con un nuovo amore
He returned, found out she was married, and with a new love

volle spegner la fiamma che gli bruciava il core.
he wished to quench the flame that consumed his heart.

M'amò, l'amai!
He loved me, I loved him (back)!

Quell'invidia d'ogni delizia mia,
That envious woman, of every joy mine,

del suo sposo dimentica, arse di gelosia.
of her husband forgets (and) is consumed by jealousy.

(That woman, jealous of my every joy, forgetting her new husband,
was consumed with jealousy.)

Me l'ha rapito!
She stole him from me!

Priva dell'onor mio rimango:
Deprived of my honor, I remain:

Lola e Turiddu s'amano, io piango!
Lola and Turiddu are lovers, I weep!

LUCIA
Miseri noi, che cosa vieni a dirmi in questo santo giorno?
Mercy on us, what come you to tell me on this holy day?

SANTUZZA
Io son dannata! Andate, o mamma, ad implorare Iddio,
I am damned! Go, oh mamma, to implore God,

e pregate per me.
and pray for me.

Verrà Turiddu, vo' supplicarlo un'altra volta ancora!
Will come Turiddu, I will beg him one more time again!
(Turiddu will soon come; I will beg him one more time!)

LUCIA
Aiutatela voi, Santa Maria!
Help her, (Thou) Holy Mary!

(Lucia va in chiesa. Quasi immediatamente Turiddu entra.)
(Lucia goes into the church. Almost immediately Turiddu enters.)

TURIDDU
Tu qui, Santuzza?
You here, Santuzza?

SANTUZZA
Qui t'aspettavo.
Here I was waiting for you.

TURIDDU
È Pasqua, in chiesa non vai?
It's Easter, to church you are not going?

SANTUZZA
Non vo . . . debbo parlarti.
I'm not going . . . I must talk to you.

TURIDDU
Mamma cercavo.
Mamma I was looking for.

SANTUZZA
Debbo parlarti.

TURIDDU
Qui no!
Here no!
(Not here!)

SANTUZZA
Dove sei stato?
Where have you been?

TURIDDU
Che vuoi tu dire . . . a Francofonte.

What do you mean . . . in Francofonte.

SANTUZZA
No, non è ver.
No, it isn't true.

TURIDDU
Santuzza, credimi.
Santuzza, believe me.

SANTUZZA
No, non mentire. Ti vidi volger giù dal sentier.
No, don't lie. I saw you turning off from the path.

E stamattina all'alba t'hanno scorto presso l'uscio di Lola.
And this morning at dawn you were seen near the doorway of Lola.

TURIDDU
(arrabbiato)
(angry)
Ah! Mi hai spiato!
Ah! You were spying on me!

SANTUZZA
No! Te lo giuro,
No! I swear to you,

a noi l'ha raccontato compar Alfio, il marito poco fa.
to us it told neighbor Alfio her husband just now.
(her husband Alfio told us just now.)

TURIDDU
Cosi ricambi l'amor che ti porto? Vuoi che m'uccida?
Thus you repay the love that I bear you? Do you want that he kill me?

SANTUZZA
Oh! Questo non lo dire!
Oh! This you musn't say!
    (Don't say that!)

TURIDDU
Lasciami dunque! Invan tenti sopire
Leave me then! In vain you try to quench
(Leave me alone!)

il giusto sdegno colla tua pietà.
my rightful anger with your pity.

SANTUZZA
Tu l'ami dunque?
You love her, then?

TURIDDU
No!

SANTUZZA
(sarcastico)
(sarcastically)
Assai più bella[9] è Lola . . .
Much more beautiful is Lola . . .

TURIDDU
Taci! Non l'amo!
Be quiet! I don't love her!

SANTUZZA
L'ami, o maledetto!
You love her, oh cursed man!

TURIDDU
Santuzza!

SANTUZZA
Quella cattiva femmina ti tolse a me!
That evil female took you away from me!

TURIDDU
Bada, Santuzza, schiavo non sono di questa vana tua gelosia.
Mind, Santuzza, a slave I'm not of this useless your jealousy.
(See here, Santuzza, I won't be a slave to your useless jealousy.)

SANTUZZA
Battimi, insultami, t'amo e perdono,
Beat me, insult me, I love you and I forgive you,

ma è troppo forte l'angoscia mia.
but it is too strong my anguish.
(but my anguish is unbearable.)

TURIDDU
Bada, Santuzza, schiavo non sono, etc.

SANTUZZA
Battimi, insultami, etc.

(Sentendo la voce di Lola che s'avvicina cantando, i due tacciono d'improvviso.)
(They stop their argument as they hear Lola's voice singing off stage.)

LOLA
(dentro alla scena)
(offstage)

Fior di giaggiolo,
Flower of iris,

gli angeli belli stanno a mille in cielo,
the angels beautiful are by thousands in heaven,
(there are beautiful angels by the thousands in heaven,)

ma bello come lui ce n'è uno solo!
but beautiful like it there is one only!
(but there is no angel as beautiful as the iris flower!)[10]

Fior di giaggiolo . . .

(Lei entra in vista.)
(She comes into view.)

Oh! . . . Turiddu È passato Alfio?
Oh! . . . Turiddo, has passed Alfio?
                 (has Alfio been through here?)

TURIDDU
(imbarazzato)
(embarrassed)
Son giunto ora in piazza . . . non so.
I've arrived just now on the plaza . . . I don't know.

LOLA
Forse è rimasto dal maniscalco, ma non può tardare . . .
Maybe he has stayed at the blacksmith's, but he can't be long . . .

E voi, sentite le funzioni in piazza?
And you two, will you hear the service out (on the) plaza?

TURIDDU
Santuzza mi narrava . . .
Santuzza was telling me . . .

SANTUZZA
(tetra)
(bitterly)
Gli dicevo che oggi è Pasqua e il Signor vede ogni cosa!
I was telling him that today is Easter and the Lord sees everything.

LOLA
Non venite alla messa?
Aren't you coming to Mass?

SANTUZZA
(con intento malevolo)
(with malicious intention)
Io no, ci deve andar chi sa di non aver peccato!
Not I. There should go who knows of not having sinned!
(Only those who haven't sinned should go to Mass!)

LOLA
Io ringrazio il Signore, e bacio in terra!
I thank the Lord, and kiss the ground!

SANTUZZA
Oh, fate bene, Lola!
Oh, you do well, Lola!

TURIDDU
(a Lola)
(to Lola)
Andiamo. Qui non abbiam che fare.

Let's go. Here we haven't what to do.
　　　　(There's nothing to do here.)

LOLA
(a Turiddu, con ironia)
(to Turiddu, with irony)
Oh, rimanete . . .
Oh, stay . . .

SANTUZZA
(a Turiddu)
(to Turiddu)
Sì, resta, ho da parlarti ancora.
Yes, stay, I have to talk to you further.

LOLA
E v'assista il Signore. Io me ne vado.
And be with you the Lord. I am leaving.

(Entra in chiesa.)
(Lola goes into the church.)

TURIDDU
Ah! Lo vedi, che hai tu detto?
Ah! You see, what have you said?

SANTUZZA
L'hai voluto, e ben ti sta!
You asked for it, and well you deserve it!

TURIDDU
(minacciare il suo)
(threatening her)
Ah! per Dio!

Ah! By God!

SANTUZZA
Squarciami il petto . . .
Tear out my breast . . .
(Tear out my heart!)

TURIDDU
(s'avvia)
(turning to go)
No!
No!

SANTUZZA
Turiddu, ascolta!
Turiddu, listen!

TURIDDU
Va!
Go!

SANTUZZA
Turiddu, ascolta!

No, Turiddu, rimani ancora! abbandonarmi dunque tu vuoi?
No, Turiddu, stay a bit longer! To forsake me then you want?

TURIDDU
Perchè seguirmi . . .
Why follow me . . .

SANTUZZA
No, Turiddu . . .

TURIDDU
Perchè spiarmi . . . sul limitare fin della chiesa?
Why spy on me . . . to the very entrance of the church?

SANTUZZA
La tua Santuzza piange e t'implora;
Your Santuzza weeps and is begging you;

come cacciarla così tu puoi?
how send her away thus you can?

TURIDDU
Va, ti ripeto . . . non tediarmi!
Go, I tell you again . . . don't pester me!

SANTUZZA
No, Turiddu, rimani ancora, etc.

Pentirsi è vano dopo l'offesa.
To be sorry is useless after the offense.
(It's too late to be sorry.)

SANTUZZA
(con voce terribilmente angosciata)
(in a terrifyingly anguished voice)
Bada!
Beware!

TURIDDU
Dell'ira tua non mi curo!
Over the anger yours I don't give a damn!

(La getta a terra e fugge in chiesa.)
(He throws her down and escapes into the church.)

SANTUZZA
(nel colmo dell'ira)
(in utter rage, calling after him)
A te la mala Pasqua, spergiuro!
To you a bad Easter, deceiver!
(And may your Easter be cursed, deceiver!)

(Cade affranta ed angosciata. Entra in scena Alfio e s'incontra con Santuzza.)
(Santuzza collapses in a frenzy of grief. Alfio enters and approaches Santuzza, who then gets up.)

SANTUZZA
Oh! Il Signore vi manda, compar Alfio!
Oh! The Lord sends you, neighbor Alfio!

ALFIO
A che punto è la messa?
At what point is the Mass?

SANTUZZA
È tardi ormai, Ma per voi,
It's late now. But I must tell you,

Lola è andata con Turiddu!
Lola has gone in with Turiddu!

ALFIO
(sorpreso)
(surprised)
Che avete detto?
What did you say?

SANTUZZA
Che mentre correte all'acqua e al vento
That while you're running around in rain and in wind

a guadagnarvi il pane,
to earn yourself the bread,
(earning a living through rain and bad weather,)

Lola v'adorna il tetto in malo modo!
Lola is decorating your roof in a bad manner![11]

ALFIO
Ah, nel nome di Dio, Santa, che dite?
Ah, in the name of God, Santa, what are you saying?

SANTUZZA
Il ver . . . Turiddu mi tolse l'onore,
The truth . . . Turiddu despoiled me of my honor,

e vostra moglie lui rapiva a me!
and your wife him stole from me!

ALFIO
Se voi mentite, vo' schiantarvi il core!
If you are lying, I'll tear out your heart!

SANTUZZA
Uso a mentire il labbro mio non è!
Accustomed to lying the lip mine is not!
(I am not in the habit of lying!)

Per la vergogna mia, pel mio dolore
To the shame mine, to my grief

la triste verità vi dissi, ahimè!
the sad truth I have told you, alas!

ALFIO
Comare Santa, allor grato vi sono.
My friend Santa, then thankful I am to you.

SANTUZZA
Infame io son che vi parlai così!
Vile I am that I spoke to you thus!

ALFIO
Infami loro: ad essi non perdono, vendetta avrò
Vile (are) they; to those I won't forgive, vengeance I will have
(They are the vile ones; I will have my *vendetta*)

pria che tramonti il di.
before the end of this day.

Io sangue voglio, all'ira m'abbandono,
I blood want, to rage I abandon myself,
(I want blood, I yield to my rage,)

in odio tutto l'amor mio finì!
in hate all my love ended!
(all of my love has turned to hate!)

(Alfio insegue off. Santuzza corre disperatamente dietro inutilmente
e alla fine esce anche.)
(Alfio stalks off. Santuzza desperately runs after him to no avail and even-
tually exits also.)

INTERMEZZO

(Tutti escono di chiesa, Lucia traversa la scena ed entra in casa.)
(Everyone comes out of the church. Mamma Lucia crosses the square and goes into her house.)

UOMINI CORO
CHORUS MEN
A casa, amici ove ci aspettano le nostre donne. Andiam!
Homeward, friends, where await us our women. Let's go!

Or che letizia rasserena gli animi,
Now that happiness calms down our states of mind,

senza indugio corriam!
without delay let us run!

DONNE CORO
CHORUS WOMEN
A casa, amiche, ove ci aspettano i nostri sposi, Andiam!
Homeward, friends, where await us our husbands. Let's go!

Or che letizia rasserena gli animi, etc.

(Il coro si avvia. Turiddu e Lola escono di chiesa.)
(Lola and Turiddu come out of the church.)

TURIDDU
Comare Lola, ve ne andate via senza nemmeno salutare?
Neighbor Lola, you are going without even a word of greeting?

LOLA
Vado a casa; non ho visto compar Alfio!
I'm going home; I haven't seen neighbor Alfio!

TURIDDU
Non ci pensate, verrà in piazza.
Don't think about it, he will come to the square.
(Don't worry, he will be here soon.)

(per le persone intorno a lui)
(to the people around him)

Intanto amici, qua, beviamone un bicchiere!
Meanwhile, friends, here, let us drink a glassful!

(Tutti si avvicinano alla tavola dell'osteria e prendono i bicchieri.)
(All approach the table outside the tavern and pour themselves glasses of wine.)

Viva il vino spumeggiante nel bicchiere scintillante
Long live the wine foaming, in the glass sparkling

come il riso dell'amante mite infonde il giubilo!
as laughter from a lover meekly inspires good cheer!

Viva il vino ch'è sincero, che ci allieta ogni pensiero,
Hurrah for the wine that is honest, that gladdens for us every
thought,

a che affoga l'umor nero nell'ebbrezza tenera!
and that drowns the humor black in merriment gentle!
(and drowns the blackest mood in gentle merriment!)

UOMINI CORO
CHORUS MEN
Viva!

TURIDDU
(a Lola)

(to Lola)
Ai vostri amori.
To your loves.

(Beve.)
(He drinks.)

LOLA
(a Turiddu)
(to Turiddu)
Alla fortuna vostra!
To the good fortune yours!

(Beve.)
(She drinks.)

UOMINI CORO
CHORUS MEN
Viva!

TURIDDU
Beviam!
Let's drink!

UOMINI E DONNE CORO
CHORUS MEN AND WOMEN
Beviam! Rinnovisi la giostra!
Let's drink! Let's go on with the merrymaking!

TURIDDU, LOLA, CORO
TURIDDU, LOLA, CHORUS
Beviam! Rinnovisi la giostra! Viva il vino spumeggiante!

CORO
CHORUS
Viva il vin!
Long live the wine!

*(**Alfio appare in piazza.**)*
(Alfio appears in the square.)

ALFIO
A voi tutti, salute!
To all of you, greetings!

CORO
CHORUS
Compar Alfio, salute!
Neighbor Alfio, greetings!

TURIDDU
Benvenuto!
Welcome!

*(**Empie un bicchiere.**)*
(He fills a glass.)

Con noi dovete bere, ecco, pieno è il bicchiere!
With us you must drink, here, full is the glass!

ALFIO
(respingendolo)
(pushing the glass away)
Grazie, ma il vostro vino io non l'accetto;
Thanks, but your wine I won't accept;

diverrebbe veleno entro il mio petto!

it would become poison inside my breast!
>   (stomach!)

TURIDDU
(getta il vino)
(throwing the wine away)
A piacer vostro.
At pleasure yours.
(Just as you like.)

LOLA
Ahimè, che mai sarà?
Alas, what will happen?

(Alcune donne, dopo una consultazione sussurrata, avvicinano Lola.)
(Some women, after a whispered consultation, approach Lola.)

DONNE CORO
CHORUS WOMEN
Comare Lola, andiamo via di qua.
Friend Lola, let us get away from here.

(Tutte le donne lasciano, prendendo Lola con loro.)
(All the women leave, taking Lola with them.)

TURIDDU
(a Alfio)
(to Alfio)
Avete altro a dirmi?
Have you anything else to tell me?

ALFIO
Io? Nulla!
I? Nothing!

TURIDDU
Allora sono agli ordini vostri.
Then I am at the orders yours.
(Then I am at your service.)

ALFIO
Or ora?
Right now?

TURIDDU
Or ora!
Right now!

(Alfio e Turiddu si abbracciano. Turiddu morde l'orecchio destro di
Aifio in sfida, secondo le regole siciliane di sfida.)
(Alfio and Turiddu embrace. Turiddu bites Alfio's right ear in defiance,
according to the Sicilian rules of challenge.)

ALFIO
Compar Turiddu, avete morso a buono;
Neighbor Turiddu, you've bitten to good effect;

c'intenderemo bene, a quel che pare.
we will understand each other well, as it would seem.

TURIDDU
Compar Alfio . . . lo so che il torto è mio,
Neighbor Alfio . . . I know that the fault is mine,
                    (I know that I am in the wrong,)

e ve lo giuro nel nome di Dio
and I swear to you in the name of God

che al par d'un cane mi farei sgozzar . . .

that like a dog I'd let myself (by you) slit the throat . . .
(that I'd let you slit my throat like a dog . . .)

Ma s'io non vivo, resta abbandonata povera Santa!
But if I don't survive, remains deserted, (my) poor Santa!

Lei che mi s'è data . . .
She who to me gave herself . . .

Vi saprò in core il ferro[12] mio piantar!
I will in heart the dagger mine plunge!
(I will put my dagger through your heart!)

ALFIO
(freddamente)
(coldly)
Compare, fate come più vi piace;
My friend, do as you like;

Io v'aspetto qui fuori dietro l'orto.
I will wait for you here outside behind the orchard.

TURIDDU
(andando a sua madre dopo Alfio ha lasciato)
(going to his mother after Alfio has left)
Mamma, quel vino è generoso, e certo oggi,
Mamma, that wine is heady, and for sure today,

troppi bicchieri ne ho tracannati. Vado fuori all'aperto . . .
too many glasses of it I guzzled. I am going outside in the open . . .

Ma prima voglio che mi benedite
But first I want that you bless me

come quel giorno che partii soldato.
like that day when I left as a soldier.

Eppoi, Mamma, sentite, s'io non tornassi,
And then, Mamma, listen, if I shouldn't return,

voi dovrete fare da madre a Santa,
you must be like a mother to Santa,

ch'io l'avea giurato di condurla all'altare.
for I had to her sworn to lead her to the altar.

LUCIA
Perchè parli così, figliolo mio?
Why do you speak like that, my son?

TURIDDU
Oh! nulla . . . è il vino che mi ha suggerito!
Oh! Nothing . . . it's the wine that gave me these ideas!

Per me pregate Iddio, un bacio, mamma!
For me pray (to) God, a kiss, mamma!

Un altro bacio . . . addio! S'io non tornassi
Another kiss . . . farewell! If I weren't to come back

fate da madre a Santa; un bacio, addio!
be a mother to Santa; a kiss, farewell!

(L'abbraccia ed esce precipitosamente.)
(He embraces his mother, kisses her, and rushes out.)

LUCIA
(disperata correndo in fondo)

(desperately running after him)
Turiddu! . . . Che vuoi dire? Turiddu! Ah!
Turiddu! . . . What do you mean? Turiddu! Ah!

(Entra Santuzza.)
(Santuzza enters.)

Santuzza!

SANTUZZA
(abbracciare Lucia)
(embracing Lucia)
Oh, madre mia!
Oh, my mother!

(Gli abitanti del villaggio di ritorno, tutti in uno stato di grande agitazione, con espressioni di paura sui loro volti.)
(The villagers return, all in a state of great agitation, with expressions of fear on their faces.)

VOCE DI DONNA
WOMAN'S VOICE
(correndo)
(offstage)
Hanno ammazzato compare Turiddu!
They've killed neighbor Turiddu!

SANTUZZA
Ah!

FINE DELL'OPERA
END OF THE OPERA

Ruggero Leoncavallo's
Pagliacci

Synopsis

Prologue

Tonio the clown announces that what the audience is about to see is a true story and that actors have the same joys and sorrows as other people.

Act I

A village in Calabria, southern Italy. A small theatrical company has just arrived, and Canio, the head of the troupe, advertises the night's performance to the gathered crowd. One of the villagers suggests that Tonio is secretly courting Canio's young wife, Nedda. Canio warns them all that he will not tolerate any flirting offstage—life and theater are not the same. As the crowd disperses, Nedda is left alone, disturbed by her husband's jealousy. She looks up to the sky, envying the birds their freedom. Tonio appears and tries to force himself on her, but she beats him back and he retreats, swearing revenge. In fact, Nedda does have a lover—Silvio, a young peasant, who suddenly appears. The two reaffirm their love and Silvio persuades Nedda to run away with him that night. Tonio, who has returned and overheard the end of their conversation, hurries off to alert Canio, but Silvio manages to slip away unrecognized. Canio violently threatens Nedda, but she refuses to reveal her lover's name. Beppe, another member of the troupe, restrains Canio, and

Tonio advises him to wait until the evening's performance to catch the culprit. Alone, Canio gives in to his despair—he must play the clown even though his heart is breaking.

Act II

That evening, the villagers assemble to watch the performance, Silvio among them. Beppe plays Harlequin, who serenades Columbine, played by Nedda. He dismisses her buffoonish servant, Taddeo, played by Tonio, and over dinner the two sweethearts plot to poison Columbine's husband, Pagliaccio, played by Canio. When Pagliaccio unexpectedly appears, Harlequin slips away. Taddeo maliciously assures Pagliaccio of his wife's innocence, which ignites Canio's jealousy. Forgetting his role and the play, he demands that Nedda tell him the name of her lover. She tries to continue with the performance, the audience enthralled by its realism, until Canio snaps. In a fit of rage, he stabs Nedda and then Silvio, who rushes to her aid. Turning to the horrified crowd, Canio announces that the comedy is over.

In Focus

William Berger

Premiere: Teatro dal Verme, Milan
May 21, 1892

Pagliacci is a tale of jealousy and murder among a troupe of traveling clowns, a look at the intersection of art and life so definitive that
it has in many people's minds come to represent all opera. Written
hot on the heels of the success of Mascagni's *Cavalleria Rusticana*,
Pagliacci consciously utilizes the same verismo techniques in its
musical and dramatic core and yet remains a distinct and equally
powerful work of theater. While *Cavalleria* reveled in the realism
of a village whose mores were unchanged since pre-history, the
drama of *Pagliacci* found a way to expand the narrative vision
of the verismo movement: the second half of the opera is a sort
of play-within-a-play, and the frivolity of the subject of adultery
in the traditional *commedia dell'arte* presentation of the traveling
clowns becomes one of the driving forces of the climactic murder. By
drawing this sort of a narrative frame around the on-stage action,
Leoncavallo could harness all its irony, tradition, and symbolism
while remaining firmly in realism, and using the artifice of theater
to emphasize, rather than obscure, the truth of human emotion.
Pagliacci, no less than *Cavalleria*, has seared itself onto the commu-
nal consciousness well beyond the opera house, and the poignant

image of the clown working to make an audience laugh while in a state of despair reverberates to the present day.

The Creator

Ruggero Leoncavallo (1857–1919) studied music in his native Naples and became an ardent admirer of Richard Wagner. He wrote all his own libretti, as Wagner had, and had a checkered, rather picaresque career from Cairo to Berlin. Along with several others, he contributed to the libretto of Puccini's hit *Manon Lescaut* before the two parted ways. The most notable wedge between them came when Puccini declared he was setting *La Bohème* as an opera, after Leoncavallo had already announced the same intention to the press. Both were successfully staged, and although Puccini's has become one of the world's most popular operas, Leoncavallo's is still heard on occasion and has received some lasting attention. In fact, several of Leoncavallo's other works have received ongoing acclaim in Italy, but the composer's international reputation rests squarely on his youthful verismo hit.

The Setting

Pagliacci is set in a village in Calabria in southern Italy around 1865. In the mid-19th century, traveling troupes of *commedia dell'arte* players, interpreting the stock characters of Harlequin, Columbine, and others, were a familiar feature of this landscape. The specified time is the Feast of the Assumption (August 15), a major holiday in Italy. The current Met production moves the setting to the late 1940s, creating a sense that the story is taking place in the same village as *Cavalleria Rusticana*, two generations later.

The Music

In some ways, the score of *Pagliacci* expresses verismo ideals even more impressively than *Cavalleria*, most notably in the unity of each scene and the seamless transitions between individual solos. After some early scene painting (including the pretty bell chorus), there is scarcely a line of music that does not advance the swift action of the drama. The soprano's aria, "Stridono lassù," shows that even verismo works demand beauty of tone. Likewise, Harlequin's serenade requires elegant phrasing, especially since it is delivered within the framework of a play-within-a-play. Tonio's opening prologue, "Si può?," a daunting solo traditionally delivered in front of the curtain, is a magnificent tour de force for the baritone (and a superb dramatic touch). There is, as in *Cavalleria*, a powerful orchestral intermezzo, but *Pagliacci* is most noted for its Act I climax, the tenor aria "Vesti la giubba," one of the world's most familiar melodies. It was, in Caruso's rendition, the recording industry's first million-seller.

Cavalleria Rusticana and *Pagliacci* at the Met

Cavalleria was first performed by the Met on tour in Chicago in December 1891, paired with Act I of Verdi's *La Traviata*. *Pagliacci* followed in December 1893 at the opera house in New York, in a double bill with Gluck's *Orfeo ed Euridice*. The Met was the first opera company to present *Cav/Pag* together on December 22, 1893 (with *Pagliacci* performed first), but occasional pairings with other operas were still common into the early 20th century. *Cavalleria* and *Pagliacci* individually shared the Met stage with such diverse works as *Il Barbiere di Siviglia*, *Don Pasquale*, *Lucia di Lammermoor*, *La Fille du Régiment*, *Il Trovatore*, *Rigoletto*, *La Bohème*, and even Rimsky-Korsakov's *Le Coq d'Or*. An unlikely double bill of *Pagliacci* and *Hansel and Gretel* was especially popular, with almost 100 performances between 1906 and 1938. Among the notable early interpreters of the leading roles were Emma Eames, Emma Calvé, Johanna Gadski, Olive Fremstad, Emmy Destinn, and Rosa Ponselle (Santuzza); Francesco Tamagno and Enrico Caruso (Turiddu); Nellie Melba, Destinn, Lucrezia Bori, Claudia Muzio, and Queena Mario (Nedda); Caruso (more than 100 performances) and Giovanni Martinelli (Canio); and Pasquale Amato (Tonio). A new production in 1951 starred Zinka Milanov and Richard Tucker in *Cavalleria* and Delia Rigal, Ramón Vinay, and Leonard Warren in *Pagliacci*. This was succeeded by another new staging in 1958, with Lucine Amara as Nedda, Mario Del Monaco as Canio, and Milanov and Warren reprising their roles. The following production, directed and designed by Franco Zeffirelli, premiered in 1970 with Leonard Bernstein conducting a cast that included Grace Bumbry and Franco Corelli in *Cavalleria* and Amara, Richard Tucker, and Sherrill Milnes in *Pagliacci*. Among the many other artists who have appeared in the two operas since the late 1950s are Giulietta Simionato, Eileen Farrell, Fiorenza Cossotto, and Tatiana Troyanos (Santuzza); Teresa Stratas and Diana Soviero (Nedda); Jon Vickers, James McCracken, and Giuseppe Giacomini (Canio); and Cornell MacNeil and Juan Pons (Tonio). Tenors who have faced the challenge of taking on both leading roles in the same performance include Plácido Domingo, Roberto Alagna, and José Cura. The Met's latest new production, directed by David McVicar, opens in April 2015 with Eva-Maria Westbroek as Santuzza, Patricia Racette as Nedda, and Marcelo Álvarez singing Turiddu and Canio.

Program Note

Richard Dyer

In 1888 Pietro Mascagni was a failure. His father was a respectable journeyman baker who didn't want any musicians in the family, but the young Mascagni had gone to the Milan Conservatory anyway. He didn't like it, though, finding the disciplines of counterpoint and fugue not suited to his temperament. He soon left to become a conductor in an itinerant opera company, and when that folded he settled in a small town and gave piano lessons.

Then the publishing house of Sonzogno arranged a contest for one-act operas. Mascagni turned to a work of Giovanni Verga's—the short story *Cavalleria Rusticana*, which had been adapted as a play—and within a few short months wrote an opera. It beat out 72 other contestants and had its triumphant premiere in Rome in 1890. Even the aged Verdi, who had written *Otello* but not yet *Falstaff*, conceded that *Cavalleria Rusticana* wasn't bad: "It has all the elements of success." Although Mascagni lived until 1945 and wrote more than a dozen other operas, his reputation still rests on his early masterpiece, composed when he was 25.

Some time after *Cavalleria*'s premiere, another unsuccessful young man who was earning his living as an accompanist and café pianist set out to try his hand at a similar work. Ruggero Leoncavallo's *Pagliacci* opened at the Teatro dal Verme in Milan in May 1892, two years after *Cavalleria*, creating the same kind of sensation. The following year, the Met was the first opera company to present the two works together in one evening—a pairing that soon became standard practice.

In the 1890s both *Cavalleria* and *Pagliacci* were thought to represent something new: Tonio, in the familiar prologue to Leoncavallo's opera, goes a way toward telling us what. He appears in front of the curtain to reassure us that this is not just a story; instead he's bringing us a slice of life. (In fact, Leoncavallo claimed, almost certainly falsely, that he had taken his story from an actual court case that his father, a magistrate, had tried.) We will see human passions as they work themselves out in the real world, Tonio continues—love and hatred, woe, howlings of rage, and scornful laughter.

Of course, opera had depicted such emotions for a long, long time—all of these elements occur in Mozart's *Don Giovanni*, written more than 100 years earlier. What was new was the social position of the characters. With *Cav* and *Pag*, along with Bizet's *Carmen* (1875), we move away from dramas about people of noble birth acted out in remote historical settings. In early opera, the action on the stage reflected the preoccupations of the aristocratic audience; later, for audiences of a wider social range, the music served to make the emotions of remote characters accessible, to show that persons of high rank are swayed by the same passions as the audience that listens. (Though in fairness to a few other antecedents, Verdi's *Luisa Miller* is about a farmer's daughter, and though a baron and a marquis make incidental appearances, *La Traviata* is about what happens when the respectable middle class gets involved with the demi-monde.) In the music of *Cavalleria* and *Pagliacci*, we find the emotions of the lowborn ennobled, given size and importance. Characters in these operas frequent taverns and go to blacksmiths and work in the fields and rub down donkeys—and experience love and hatred, woe, howlings of rage, and scornful laughter; these are part of what Verdi meant by "the elements of success." The emphasis in the verismo genre is on the size of emotion, as a look at some of the marks of expression in the score of *Cavalleria* demonstrates: *con disperazione, con angoscia, con dolore, con amarezza* ("with bitterness"), *nel colmo dell'ira* ("at the peak of fury"), *con forza,* and, of course, *con suprema passione.*

Much has been made of the swiftness of action in these operas, and indeed there are striking, sudden transformations, mostly brought about by emotional upheaval. After the few measures of Santuzza's narrative, the affable Alfio sings that his love for Lola has turned to hatred; wildly he calls for vengeance and blood. Alfio and Turiddu go off together, and a moment later a peasant woman screams that Turiddu has been killed; Canio erupts and sings that he is no longer a clown. What Shaw wrote of *Cavalleria* is equally true of its partner: the opera, he said, is "a youthfully vigorous piece of work, with abundant snatches of melody broken obstreperously off on one dramatic pretext or another."

But it is also necessary to observe that at the same time both operas are slow-moving, traditional pieces, with arias, duets, and choruses formally worked out, before being broken "obstreperously" off. The Easter chorus and drinking song in *Cavalleria*, the bell chorus and Nedda's aria in *Pagliacci*, may tell us a little about character, but mostly they sketch in background and atmosphere, and a very prettified version of peasant life it is. *Cavalleria*, in fact, is nearly half over before anything much happens and, oddly, even then most of the real action occurs offstage. For all the violence of the emotions the music depicts, we see only an ear getting bitten. But all the atmospheric musical genre-painting is what gives the culminating events their context and much of their effect: the swiftness of the tragic action is like the swiftness of most of the crucial events in real life, rudely intruding on the ordinariness of the daily.

Critics have always tended to condescend to these operas, especially to *Cavalleria*. And it is true that the emotions in Mascagni's opera are uncomplicated, the tunes sturdy and simple, the orchestration borderline crude. *Pagliacci* is more sophisticated dramatically and musically in its exploitation of the perennial theme of theatrical illusion and reality. But each of the operas has had diverse and even surprising admirers—Puccini, of course, but also Massenet, Debussy, Sibelius, even Gustav Mahler. And for more than 120 years the loyalty of the public has never once wavered. That's the kind of prolonged success it's hard to argue with.

C. MISHKIN
N.Y. 18

Rosa Ponselle as Santuzza, 1921
HERMAN MISHKIN / METROPOLITAN OPERA ARCHIVES

The Met's first televised performance, broadcast live from
NBC Studios on March 10, 1940, featured excerpts from Act I
of *Pagliacci* with Armand Tokatyan as Canio and Frank St. Leger
conducting the NBC Orchestra, along with selections from
Carmen, *La Gioconda*, *Il Barbiere di Siviglia*, and *Rigoletto*.
METROPOLITAN OPERA ARCHIVES

Giovanni Martinelli as Canio, 1941
METROPOLITAN OPERA ARCHIVES

Licia Albanese as Nedda, 1943
METROPOLITAN OPERA ARCHIVES

Director Hans Busch, at left, with Jean Madeira (Mamma Lucia in *Cavalleria*) and Frank Guarrera (Silvio in *Pagliacci*) during a rehearsal break for the 1951 production

Hans Busch rehearses Zinka Milanov as Santuzza, 1951.
SEDGE LEBLANG / METROPOLITAN OPERA ARCHIVES

Mario Del Monaco as Canio, 1958
GJON MILI / METROPOLITAN OPERA ARCHIVES

**Mario Sereni as Silvio and Lucine Amara as Nedda
in rehearsal for the 1958 production**
GJON MILI / METROPOLITAN OPERA ARCHIVES

Leonard Warren as Tonio, 1958
GJON MILI / METROPOLITAN OPERA ARCHIVES

Jan Peerce as Turiddu and Giulietta Simionato as
Santuzza, 1959
Louis Melançon / Metropolitan Opera Archives

Joann Grillo as Lola, Arturo Sergi as Turiddu, and Eileen Farrell as Santuzza, 1964

Set designs by Franco Zeffirelli for the 1970 production
(*Cavalleria Rusticana*, top; *Pagliacci*, bottom)

Grace Bumbry as Santuzza and Franco Corelli as Turiddu, 1970
FRANK DUNAND / METROPOLITAN OPERA ARCHIVES

Cornell MacNeil as Tonio, 1970
Frank Dunand / Metropolitan Opera Archives

**Fiorenza Cossotto as Santuzza and Plácido Domingo
as Turiddu, 1970**
Frank Dunand / Metropolitan Opera Archives

Teresa Stratas as Nedda, 1970
Frank Dunand / Metropolitan Opera Archives

Carlo Bergonzi as Turiddu, 1971
FRANK DUNAND / METROPOLITAN OPERA ARCHIVES

Richard Tucker as Canio, 1974
FRANK DUNAND / METROPOLITAN OPERA ARCHIVES

James McCracken as Canio, 1986
METROPOLITAN OPERA ARCHIVES

Diana Soviero as Nedda, 1994
ERIKA DAVIDSON / METROPOLITAN OPERA ARCHIVES

Maria Guleghina as Santuzza, 2006
MARTY SOHL / METROPOLITAN OPERA

Lado Ataneli as Tonio, 2006
MARTY SOHL / METROPOLITAN OPERA

Waltraud Meier as Santuzza and Roberto Alagna as Turiddu, 2009
MARTY SOHL / METROPOLITAN OPERA

José Cura as Canio and Nuccia Focile as Nedda, 2009
KEN HOWARD / METROPOLITAN OPERA

Scenes from *Cavalleria Rusticana* (top, 2006) and *Pagliacci*
(bottom, 2009) in Franco Zeffirelli's 1970 production

PAGLIACCI

(Strolling Players)

PERSONAGGI

Canio, capo della compagnia (nella commedia Pagliaccio): tenore
Nedda, attrice da fiera, moglie di . . . (nella commedia Colombina):
soprano
Tonio, lo scemo (nella commedia Taddeo): baritono
Silvio, campagnuolo: baritone
Beppe, commediante (nella commedia Arlecchino): tenore

CHARACTERS

Canio ("Pagliaccio" in the play), leader of a troupe of strolling
players: tenor
Nedda ("Colombina" in the play), his wife and leading lady: soprano
Tonio ("Taddeo" in the play), a somewhat deformed clown: baritone
Silvio, a villager, secret lover of Nedda: baritone
Beppe ("Arlecchino" in the play), the juvenile lead: tenor

*La scena si passa in Calabria presso Montalto, il giorno della festa
di Mezzagosto. Epoca presente, fra il 1865 e il 1870.*
*The action takes place in Montalto, Calabria. The time is 1865–70 on the
Feast of the Assumption on August 15th.*

ATTO PRIMO
ACT I

(Durante il preludio del buffone Tonio sporge la testa tra le tende chiedendo di essere ascoltato. Poi parti le tende e arriva sul palco dicendo che è il prologo.)
(During the prelude the fool Tonio pokes his head through the curtains, begging to be heard. He then parts the curtains and comes on stage saying that he is the prologue.)

ARIA—PROLOGO
ARIA—PROLOGUE

TONIO
Si può? Signore, signori, scusatemi se da sol mi presento.
May I? Ladies, gentlemen, forgive me if present myself.

Io sono il prologo:
I am the Prologue;

poichè in iscena ancor
whereas on stage again

le antiche maschere mette l'autore,
the old characters places the author,
(whereas the author again places the traditional characters on the stage,)

in parte ei vuol riprendere le vecchie usanze,
in part he wishes to re-introduce the old customs,

e a voi di nuovo inviami.
and to you anew he sends me.
(and [the author] sends me to you anew.)

Ma non per dirvi come pria:
But not to tell you as before:

"Le lacrime che noi versiam son false!
"The tears that we shed are false!

Degli spasimi e dei nostri martir non allarmatevi!"
Over our anguish and of our suffering do not be alarmed!"

No! . . . L'autore ha cercato invece pingervi
No! . . . The author has sought instead to depict for you

uno squarcio di vita.
a slice of life.

Egli ha per massima sol che l'artista è un uom,
He has for a maxim only that the artist is a man,

e che per gli uomini scrivere ei deve,
and that for men write he must,

ed al vero ispiravasi.
and from truth he drew inspiration.

Un nido di memorie in fondo a l'anima
A nest of memories in the depths of his soul

cantava un giorno,
sang one day,
(Memories, like fledglings in a nest, sang in his heart's depths one day,)

ed ei con vere lacrime scrisse,
and he with real tears wrote,

e i singhiozzi il tempo gli battevano!
and the sobs the rhythm beat for him!
(and sobs were the beat of his rhythm!)

Dunque, vedrete amar, siccome s'amano gli esseri umani;
Thus, you will see loving, as love one another the beings human;
(Thus, the love that you will see is the love of human beings;)

vedrete dell'odio i tristi frutti;
you will see of hate the sad fruits;
(you will see the tragic fruits of hate;)

del dolor gli spasimi, urli di rabbia udrete
of pain the cries, yells of rage you'll hear

e risa ciniche!
and laughter cynical!

E voi, piuttosto che le nostre povere gabbane d'istrioni
And you, rather than our poor trappings of actors

le nostr'anime considerate, poichè siam uomini di carne e d'ossa
our souls give consideration, since we are men of flesh and bone
(But you, dear public, rather than to our poor theatrical trappings,
give consideration to our souls, for we are men of flesh and bone)

e che di quest'orfano mondo al pari di voi spiriamo l'aere!
and that of this God-forsaken world like you breathe the air!
(who, just as you do, breathe the air in this God-forsaken world
of ours!)

Il concetto vi dissi . . . ora ascoltate com'egli è svolto.
The concept I've explained to you . . . now listen to how it develops.

(chiamata verso il fondo della scena)
(calling towards the back of the stage)

Andiam, incominciate!
Let's go, begin!

(Si sentono squilli di tromba stonata alternantisi con dei colpi di cassa, ed insieme risate, grida allegre, fischi di monelli e vociare che vanno appressandosi. Attirati dal suono I contadini di ambo i sessi in abito da festa accorrono, mentre Tonio, annoiato dalla folla che arriva, si sdraia dinanzi al teatro. Son tre ore dopo mezzogiorno, il sol d'agosto splende cocente.)
(He disappears behind the curtain. The curtain opens to reveal a clearing on the outskirts of a Calabrian village. It is early afternoon on a sunny mid-August day. To one side there is the wagon of a small travelling company, and the sound of a trumpet can be heard alternating with the beating of a bass drum. Attracted by the music and the noise, villagers dressed in holiday finery appear from all sides.)

PAESANI
VILLAGERS
(uomini e donne, variamente)
(men and women, variously)
Son qua! Ritornano! Pagliaccio è là!
They're here! They have returned! Pagliaccio is there!

Tutti lo seguono, grandi e ragazzi,
All are following him, grownups and children,

ai motti, ai lazzi applaude ognun.
his quips, his jests applauds everyone.
(everyone is applauding his quips and jests.)

Ed egli, serio, saluta e passa
And he, serious, bows and passes by

e torna a battere sulla gran cassa.
and again starts to pound on the big bass drum.

Già fra le strida i monelli
Already amid the shouting the scamps

in aria gittano i cappelli! . . .
into the air throw their hats! . . .

RAGAZZI
BOYS
Ehi! Sferza l'asino, bravo, Arlecchino!
Hey! Whip the donkey, that's it, Arlecchino!

CANIO
(dal retro della folla)
(from the back of the crowd)
Itene al . . . diavolo!
Go to the . . . devil!

BEPPE
To! Birichino!
Watch it! You rascal!

UOMINI
MEN
Gittano in aria i cappelli . . . i lor cappelli diggià.
They are throwing into the air their hats . . . their hats already.

DONNE
WOMEN
Fra strida e sibili diggià.
Amid shouting and whistling already.

(I ragazzi sembrano correre, seguendo l'asino-carrello su cui Canio e Nedda stanno cavalcando.)
(The boys appear running, following the donkey-cart on which Canio and Nedda are riding.)

UOMINI E DONNE
MEN AND WOMEN
(variamente)
(variously)
Ecco il carretto! . . . Indietro . . . Arrivano! . . . Che diavoleria,
There's the donkey-cart! . . . Stand back! . . . They're coming! . . .
What a devilish uproar,

Dio benedetto! Viva Pagliaccio!
God blessed! Hurrah for Pagliaccio!

Evviva! Il principe sei dei pagliacci,
Long live! The prince you are of clowns,

i guai discacci tu co' lieto umore.
our troubles you drive away with your merry wit.

CANIO
(dal carretto, cercando di far sentire la sua voce)
(from the donkey-cart, trying to make his voice heard)
Grazie!
Thank you!

PAESANI
VILLAGERS
Evviva! Bravo!

CANIO
Vorrei . . .
I'd like to . . .

PAESANI
VILLAGERS
E lo spettacolo?
And the show?
(When is the show?)

CANIO
(battendo sul tamburo di basso per il silenzio)
(beating on the bass drum for silence)
Signori miei . . .
My ladies and gentleman . . .

PAESANI
VILLAGERS
Uh! Ci assorda! Finiscila!
Uh! He's deafening us! Stop it!

CANIO
(salutando comicamente)
(saluting comically)
Mi accordan di parlar?
Will you allow me to speak?

PAESANI
VILLAGERS
Con lui si dee cedere, tacere ed ascoltar!

With him we must give in, keep quiet and listen!

CANIO
Un grande spettacolo a ventitré ore
A grand show at twenty-three hours[1]

prepara il vostr'umile e buon servitore!
prepares your humble and good servant!

(Fa un inchino comico.)
(He makes a comical bow.)

Vedrete le smanie del bravo Pagliaccio,
You'll see the frenzy of the good Pagliaccio,

e com'ei si vendica e tende un bel laccio!
and how he revengers himself and sets a lovely trap!

Vedrete di Tonio tremar la carcassa,
You'll see of Tonio trembling the carcass,
(You'll see how Tonio's carcass trembles,)

e quale matassa d'intrighi ordirà!
and what web of intrigue he will plot!

Venite, onorateci, Signori e Signore, a ventitré ore!
Come, honor us, Gentlemen and Ladies, at seven p.m.!

PAESANI
VILLAGERS
Verremo, e tu serbaci il tuo buon umore. A ventitré ore!
We'll come, and you keep for us your good humor. Till seven o'clock!

CANIO
A ventitré ore!

(Tonio si avanza per aiutar Nedda a scender dal carretto, ma Canio, che è già saltato giù, gli dà un ceffone dicendo.)
(Tonio tries to help Nedda alight from the cart, but Canio pushes him away roughly.)

CANIO
(a Tonio)
(to Tonio)
Via di lì!
Get out of there!

(Prende Nedda tra le braccia e la solleva giù dal carro.)
(He takes Nedda in his arms and lifts her down from the cart.)

DONNE
WOMEN
(a Tonio)
(to Tonio)
Prendi questo, bel galante!
Take that, handsome swain!

(Beppe assume il carro dietro il teatro.)
(Beppe takes the cart behind the theater.)

RAGAZZI
BOYS
(fischiando)
(mocking)
Con salute!
And enjoy it!

(Tonio fa un gesto minaccioso per i ragazzi, che scorrazzano via.)
(Tonio makes a threatening gesture to the boys, who scamper away.)

TONIO
(borbottando)
(muttering to himself)
La pagherai! Brigante!
You'll pay for that! You brigand!

(Quattro o cinque abitanti del villaggio si avvicinano Canio.)
(Four or five villagers approach Canio.)

PRIMO PAESANO
FIRST VILLAGER
(a Canio)
(to Canio)
Di', con noi vuoi bevere un buon bicchiere sulla crocevia?
Say, with us do you want to drink a good glass at the crossroads?

Di', vuoi tu?
Say, do you want to?

CANIO
Con piacere.
With pleasure.

BEPPE
(riapparire)
(reappearing)
Aspettatemi, anch'io ci stò.
Wait for me, I also will go.

(Lanciare la frusta tot egli terra, Beppe si spegne a cambiare. Canio sale al teatro.)

(Throwing the whip to the ground, Beppe goes off to change. Canio goes up to the theater.)

CANIO
(chiamando verso il teatro)
(calling towards the theater)
Di', Tonio, vieni via?
Say, Tonio, are you coming?

TONIO
(da dietro)
(from behind)
Io netto il somarello. Precedetemi.
I'll rub down the donkey. Go ahead of me.

SECONDO PAESANO
SECOND VILLAGER
(scherzosamente, di Canio)
(jokingly, to Canio)
Bada, Pagliaccio, ei solo vuol restare
Watch out, Pagliaccio, he alone wants to stay

per far la corte a Nedda!
to pay (the) court to Nedda!

CANIO
(ghignando, ma con cipiglio)
(with a forced smile)
Eh! Eh! . . . Vi pare?
Eh! Eh! . . . Do you think so?

Un tal gioco, credetemi, è meglio non giocarlo con me, miei cari;
Such a joke, believe me, it's better not to play it with me, my friends;

e a Tonio e un poco a tutti or parlo!
and to Tonio and a bit to all of you now I am speaking!

Il teatro e la vita non son la stessa cosa!!
The theater and life aren't the same thing!!

E se lassù Pagliaccio sorprende la sua sposa
And if up there Pagliaccio surprises his wife
      (up on the stage)

col bel galante in camera,
with her handsome lover in her room,

fa un comico sermone,
preaches a comical sermon,

poi si calma od arrendesi ai colpi di bastone!
then calms down or submits herself to the blows from a cane!
      (or submits to being thrashed!)

Ed il pubblico applaude ridendo allegramente!
And the public applauds laughing happily!

Ma se Nedda sul serio sorprendessi,
But if Nedda in reality I were to surprise,
(But if I should in reality catch Nedda,)

altramente finirebbe la storia com'è ver che vi parlo!
in a different way would end the story as sure as I'm talking to you!
(the story would have a very different ending, as sure as I am talking to you now!)

Un tal gioco, credetemi, è meglio non giocarlo!

NEDDA
(a parte)
(aside)
Confusa io son!
Confused I am!
(I don't know what to think!)

PAESANI
VILLAGERS
(a Canio)
(to Canio)
Sul serio pigli dunque la cosa?
In all seriousness take you then the matter?

CANIO
Io!? . . . Vi pare!! Scusatemi! Adoro la mia sposa!
I!? . . . What an idea!! Forgive me! I adore my wife!

(Va a baciare Nedda sulla fronte. In lontananza si sentono il suono rustico delle cornamuse.)
(He goes to kiss Nedda on the forehead. In the distance is heard the rustic sound of the bagpipes.)

RAGAZZI, allora DONNE
BOYS, then WOMEN
I zampognari!
The pipers!

UOMINI CORO
CHORUS MEN
Verso la chiesa vanno i compari.
Towards the church are going the neighbors.

Essi accompagnano la comitiva
They are escorting the group

che a coppie al vespero sen va giuliva.
that in couples to Vespers goes happily.
(They are escorting the group which, two by two, happily makes
its way to Vespers.)

Le campane! Andiam . . .
The bells! Let us go . . .

La campana ci appella al Signore! Andiamo!
The bell summons us to the Lord! Let us go!

CANIO
Ma poi ricordatevi! A ventitré ore!
But afterwards remember! At seven p.m.!

(Scompare dietro il teatrino. Gli zampognari entrano, scortando cop-
pie di abitanti giovani e vecchi.)
(He disappears behind the little theater. The pipers enter, escorting couples
of villagers both young and old.)

DONNE
WOMEN
Dindon, suona vespero, ragazze e garzon.
Ding dong, sounds Vespers, girls and young men.

A coppie al tempio ci affrettiam.
In couples to the church let us hasten.

Diggià i culmini il sol vuol baciar.
Already the peaks the sun wants to kiss.
(The sun is already setting behind the hills.)

Le mamme ci adocchiano, attenti, compar!

The mothers are watching us, be careful, my friends!

UOMINI
MEN
Tutto irradiasi di luce e d'amor.

Everything is bathed in light and love.

CORO
CHORUS
Ah . . . Din don, ma i vecchi sorvegliano gli arditi amador!

Ah! . . . Ding dong, but the old ones watch over the bold young lovers!

*(**Le coppie si spengono. Nedda rimane insieme sul palco.**)*
(The couples go off. Nedda remains alone on stage.)

NEDDA
Qual fiamma avea nel guardo!

What flame he had in his gaze!

Gli occhi abbassai per tema ch'ei leggesse il mio pensier segreto!

My eyes I lowered out of fear that he might read my thought secret!

Oh! S'ei mi sorprendesse, brutale come egli è!

Oh! If he were to catch me, brutal as he is!

Ma basti, orvia. Son questi sogni paurosi e fole!

But enough, come. These are dreams frightful and idle fancies!

O che bel sole di mezz'agosto!

Oh, what lovely sun of mid-August!

Io son piena di vita e tutta illanguidita
I am full of life and all langurous

per arcano desìo, non so che bramo!
with a secret desire, I know not what I long for!

(Guardando in cielo.)
(She looks up at the sky.)

Oh! Che volo d'augelli, e quante strida!
Oh! What flight of birds, and what bird-calls!

Che chiedon? . . . Dove van? . . . Chissà!
What are they asking? . . . Where are they going? . . . Who knows!

La mamma mia, che la buona fortuna annunziava,
My mother, who fortunes foretold,

comprendeva il lor canto e a me bambina così cantava:
understood their bird-song and to me as a girl thus sang:

Hui! Stridono lassù liberamente
Hoo-ee! They cry up there freely

lanciati a vol come freccie, gli augel.
launched into flight as arrows the birds.
(Hoo-ee! The birds, freely launched into flight like arrows, cry
Hoo-ee.)

Disfidano le nubi e il sol cocente,
They defy the clouds and the sun scorching,

e vanno per le vie del ciel!
and fly down the paths of the sky!

Lasciateli vagar per l'atmosfera,
Let them roam through the atmosphere,

questi, assetati d'azzurro e di splendor,
they, thirsty for the blue and for light,

seguono, anch'essi, un sogno, una chimera,
they follow, also they, a dream, a vision,
(they also follow their dream and their vision,)

e vanno² fra le nubi d'or!
and fly among the clouds of gold!

Che incalzi il vento e latri la tempesta,
Let pursue the wind and howl the tempest,
(Let the wind pursue them and the tempest howl,)

con l'ali aperte san tutto sfidar;
with their wings open they know everything to defy;
(on outspread wings they defy everything;)

la pioggia, i lampi, nulla mai li arresta,
the rain, the lighting, nothing ever stops them,

e vanno sugli abissi e i mar.
and fly above the chasms and the seas.

Vanno laggiù, verso un paese strano
They flu over there, towards a land unknown

che sognan, forse, e che cercano invan.
which they dream of, maybe, and which they search for in vain.

Ma i boëmi del ciel seguon
But the Bohemians of the sky follow
(Gypsies)

l'arcano poter che li sospinge, e van e van!
the secret compulsion that drives them, and they fly and fly!

(Si rende conto che Tonio, non osservata fino ad ora, è stato a guardare lei.)
(She realizes that Tonio, unobserved till now, has been watching her.)

Sei là? Credea che te ne fossi andato!
You are there? I thought that you had gone!

TONIO
È colpa del tuo canto. Affascinato io mi beava!
It's the fault of your singing. Fascinated, I was in a state of bliss!

NEDDA
(ridendo beffardamente)
(laughing derisively)
Ah! Ah! Quanta poesia!
Ha! Ha! Such poetry!

TONIO
Non rider, Nedda!
Don't laugh, Nedda!

NEDDA
Va, va all'osteria!
Be off, go to the tavern!

TONIO
So ben che difforme, contorto son io;

I know well that deformed, twisted am I;

che desto soltanto lo scherno e l'orror.
that I arouse only scorn and horror.

Eppur ha'l pensiero un sogno, un desio,
And yet has my thought a dream, a desire,

e un palpito il cor!
and a beat my heart!
(And yet, I have dreams and desires, and my heart also beats!)

Allor che sdegnosa mi passi d'accanto
When, disdainful, you pass me by

non sai tu che pianto mi spreme il dolor!
you don't know what tears are wrung by my grief!

Perchè, mio malgrado, subito ho l'incanto,
Because, despite myself, succumbed I have to your spell,

m'ha vinto l'amor!
I've been defeated by love!

(Va vicino a lei.)
(He goes near her.)

Oh! Lasciami or dirti . . .
Oh! Let me now tell you . . .

NEDDA
(interrompendolo)
(interrupting him)
Che m'ami?

That you love me?

(Scoppia a ridere.)
(She bursts out laughing.)

Hai tempo a ridirmelo stassera, se il brami!
You have time to tell me again this evening, if you so desire!

TONIO
Nedda!

NEDDA
Stassera! Facendo le smorfie colà sulla scena!
Tonight! When you're making faces there on stage!

TONIO
Non rider, Nedda!

NEDDA
Hai tempo! . . . Facendo le smorfie colà! Ah! Ah! Ah!

TONIO
Non sai tu che pianto mi spreme il dolore! Non rider, no!

NEDDA
Per ora tal pena ti puoi risparmiar!
For now such anguish you can to yourself spare!
(For now you can spare yourself such anguish!)

TONIO
No, è qui che voglio dirtelo, e tu m'ascolterai,
No, it is here that I want to tell you, and you will listen to me,

che t'amo e ti desidero, e che tu mia sarai!

that I love you and desire you, and that you mine shall be!

NEDDA
Eh! Dite, mastro Tonio! La schiena oggi vi prude,
Hey! Say, master Tonio! Your back today is itching,

o una tirata d'orecchi è necessaria al vostro ardore?!
or a pull of ears is necessary for your ador?!
(or do I have to pull your ears to cool your ardor?!)

TONIO
Ti beffi?! Sciagurata! Per la croce di Dio!
You're mocking me?! You wretch! By the cross of God!

Bada che puoi pagarla cara!!
Watch out that you can pay for it dearly!!

NEDDA
Minacci? Vuoi che vada a chiamar Canio?
Are you threatening? Do you want that I go to call Canio?

TONIO
(muovendosi in su di lei)
(moving in on her)
Non prima ch'io ti baci!
Not before I kiss you!

NEDDA
(tirando indietro)
(pulling back)
Bada!
Watch it!

TONIO
Or tosto sarai mia!
Now soon you will be mine!

NEDDA
Miserabile!
Miserable (wretch)!

(Nedda prende la frusta lasciato sul terreno di Beppe e lo scaglia in faccia mentre si precipita per afferrarla.)
(Nedda picks up the whip left on the ground by Beppe and lashes him across the face as he rushes to grab her.)

TONIO
Ah! Per la vergin pia di mezz'Agosto, Nedda, me la pagherai!
Ah! By the virgin holy of mid-August, Nedda, you will pay me for this!
        (Assumption)

(Se ne va, agitando il pugno in modo minaccioso.)
(He leaves, shaking his fist in a threatening manner.)

NEDDA
Aspide! Va! Ti sei svelato ormai, Tonio lo scemo!
Viper! Go! You've shown yourself for now, Tonio the fool!

Hai l'animo siccome il corpo tuo difforme, lurido!
You have a soul like the body yours deformed, disgusting!

(Entra Silvio che chiama a bassa voce.)
(Silvio appears on the other side of the wall.)

SILVIO
Nedda!

NEDDA
Silvio! A quest'ora! Che imprudenza!
Silvio! At this hour! What imprudence!

SILVIO
Ah bah! Sapea ch'io non rischiavo nulla.
Ah bah! I knew that I didn't risk anything.
(I knew that I was taking no risk.)

Canio e Beppe da lunge alla taverna ho scorto!
Canio and Beppe from afar at the tavern have I espied!

Ma prudente per la macchia
But wisely by the scrub woods

a me nota qui ne venni.
to me known here I came.
(But I wisely came here through the scrub woods known to me.)

NEDDA
E ancora un poco in Tonio t'imbattevi!
And a minute sooner into Tonio you'd have bumped!

SILVIO
Oh! Tonio lo scemo!
Oh! Tonio the fool!

NEDDA
Lo scemo è da temersi! M'ama . . .
The fool is to be feared! He's in love with me . . .

SILVIO
Ah!

Ora qui me'l disse, e nel bestial delirio suo,
Just now here he told me so, and in the bestial delirium his,
(and in his bestial passion,)

baci chiedendo, ardiva correr su me!
kisses demanding, he dared run at me!

SILVIO
Per Dio!
By God!

NEDDA
Ma con la frusta del cane immondo la foga calmai!
But with the whip, of the dog filthy the passion I calmed!
(But with the whip I calmed the filthy dog's passion.)

SILVIO
(amorevolmente disegno vicino a Nedda)
(lovingly drawing close to Nedda)
E fra quest'ansie in eterno vivrai? Nedda!
And with these anxieties forever must you live? Nedda!

(Prende la mano.)
(He takes her hand.)

Decidi il mio destin, Nedda, rimani!
Decide my fate, Nedda, stay!

Tu il sai, la festa ha fin e parte ognun domani.
You know, the holiday ends and leaves everyone tomorrow.
(You know that the holiday ends tomorrow and that everyone will leave.)

E quando tu di qui sarai partita,
And when you from here shall have gone,

che addiverrà di me, della mia vita?!
what will happent to me, to my life?!

NEDDA
(spostato)
(moved)
Silvio!

SILVIO
Nedda, rispondimi. S'è ver che Canio non amasti mai,
Nedda, answer me. If it is true that Canio you did not love ever,

s'è vero che t'è in odio il ramingar
if it is true that you hate the vagabond life

e'l mestier che tu fai,
and the work that you do,

se l'immenso amor tuo una fola non è,
if the immense love yours a pretense it is not,
(and if your great love for me isn't just a sham,)

questa notte partiam, fuggi, Nedda, con me!
tonight let us leave, flee, Nedda, with me!

NEDDA
Non mi tentar! Vuoi tu perder la vita mia?
Don't tempt me! Do you want to ruin the life mine?

Taci, Silvio, non più. È deliro, è follia!
Hush, Silvio, no more. It's delirium, it's folly!

Io mi confido a te, a te cui diedi il cor.
I put my trust in you, in you to whom I gave my heart.

Non abusar di me, del mio febbrile amor!
Do not take advantage of my feverish love!

Pietà di me! E poi, chissà . . . ! Meglio è partir.
(Have) pity on me! Yet, who knows . . . ! It is better to leave.

Sta il destin contro noi, è vano il nostro dir!
Is fate against us, it is in vain our talking!
(Fate is against us, there's nothing we can say!)

Eppur dal mio cor strapparti non poss'io;
And yet from my heart tear you away I cannot;

Vivrò sol de l'amor ch'hai destato al cor mio!
I shall live only from the love that you have awakened in the heart mine!

SILVIO
Ah! Nedda! Fuggiam!
Ah! Nedda! Let us flee!

NEDDA
Non mi tentar, vuoi tu perder la vita?, etc.

SILVIO
Nedda, rimani!

NEDDA
Taci, Silvio, non più . . . è delirio, è follia!

SILVIO
Che mai sarà di me? etc.

TONIO
(che è stato spiare gli amanti, per se stesso)
(who has been spying on the lovers, to himself)
T'ho colta, sgualdrina!
I caught you, you slut!

(Se ne va lungo il percorso.)
(He goes off along the path.)

SILVIO
No! Più non m'ami!
No! No longer do you love me!
(You no longer love me!)

NEDDA
Che! Sì, t'amo!
What! Yes, I love you!

SILVIO
E parti domattina?
And you will leave tomorrow morning?

E allor perchè, di', tu m'hai stregato
And then why, say, you have bewitched me

se vuoi lasciarmi senza pietà?!
if you want to leave me without pity?!
(Tell me, why, then, did you bewitch me and wish to leave me
without pity?!)

Quel bacio tuo perchè me l'hai dato
That kiss yours why did you give me

fra spasmi ardenti di voluttà?!
amid spasms ardent of lust?!
(Why then did you kiss me with spasms of lust?!)

Se tu scordasti l'ore fugaci,
If you have forgotten the hours fleeting,

io non lo posso, e voglio ancor
I cannot, and I want more

que' spasmi ardenti, que' caldi baci
those spasms ardent, those hot kisses

che tanta febbre m'han messo in cor!
that such fever have started in my heart!

NEDDA
Nulla scordai, sconvolta e turbata
Nothing have I forgotten, distraught and perturbed

m'ha questo amor che nel guardo ti sfavilla!
has me this love that in your gaze blazes!
(I have forgotten nothing. This love that blazes in your eyes has
left me distraught and perturbed!)

Viver voglio a te avvinta, affascinata,
To live I want to you bound, held in your spell,
(I want to live bound to you and held in your spell,)

una vita d'amor, calma e tranquilla!
a life of love, calm and quiet!

A te mi dono, su me solo impera,
To you I give myself, over me alone rule,
(I give myself to you; do with me what you wish,)

ed io ti prendo e m'abbandono intera!
and I take you and surrender entirely!

Tutto scordiam!
Everything let us forget!

SILVIO
Tutto scordiam!

NEDDA
Negli occhi mi guarda, baciami! T'amo!
In the eyes look at me, kiss me! I love you!

SILVIO
Sì, ti guardo e ti bacio! T'amo!
Yes, I look at you and I kiss you! I love you!

Verrai?
Will you come?

NEDDA
Sì, baciami!
Yes, kiss me!

(Mentre gli amanti si tengono in un abbraccio voluttuoso, Canio e Tonio appaiono sul retro.)
(While the lovers are held in a voluptuous embrace, Canio and Tonio appear at the back.)

TONIO
(a Canio)
(to Canio)
Cammina adagio e li sorprenderai!
Walk slowly and you will catch them!

SILVIO
(scavalcando il muro mentre lascia)
(climbing over the wall as he leaves)
Ad alta notte laggiù mi terrò.
At dead of night down there I shall be.

Cauta discendi e mi ritroverai.
Cautiously come down and you will find me.

(Scompare.)
(He disappears.)

NEDDA
A stanotte, e per sempre tua sarò.
Till tonight, and forever yours I shall be.

CANIO
Ah!

NEDDA
(Sorpreso dal grido di Canio, ha chiamato dopo Silvio.)
(Startled by Canio's cry, she calls after Silvio.)
Fuggi!
Flee!

(Canio si getta contro il muro. Nedda cerca di trattenerlo e non vi è una breve lotta prima Canio finalmente la spinge via e insegue l'amante di sua moglie.)

(Canio throws himself at the wall. Nedda tries to hold him back and there is a brief struggle before Canio finally pushes her away and runs after his wife's lover.)

Aiutalo . . . Signor!
Help him . . . Lord!

CANIO
Vile! T'ascondi!
Coward! You're hiding!

(Tonio ride beffardamente.)
(Tonio laughs derisively.)

NEDDA
(a Tonio)
(to Tonio)
Bravo, il mio Tonio!
Well done, my Tonio!

TONIO
Fo quel che posso!
I do what I can!

NEDDA
È quello che pensavo.
That is what I thought.

TONIO
Ma di fai assai meglio non dispero!
But of doing much better I don't despair!
(But I hope to do even better!)

NEDDA
Mi fai schifo e ribrezzo!
You cause me revolt and disgust!
(You give me revulsion and disgust!)

TONIO
Oh, non sai come lieto ne son!
Oh, you don't know how happy I am about it!

(Canio ritorna, asciugandosi il sudore.)
(Out of breath Canio comes back in, mopping his brow.)

CANIO
Derisione e scherno! Nulla!
Derision and ridicule! Nothing!
(I've been derided and fooled! Nothing!)

Ei ben lo conosce quel sentier.
He well knows it, that path.

Fa lo stesso; poichè del drudo il nome or mi dirai.
No matter; as long as of your lover the name now you tell me.

NEDDA
Chi?
Who?

CANIO
Tu, pel Padre Eterno!
You, by the Father Eternal!
(You, by God!)

E se in questo momento qui scannata non t'ho già,
And if in this instant here cut your throat I haven't you already,

(And the only reason I haven't cut your throat yet,)

(Cavando dalla cinta lo stiletto.)
(He takes out his dagger.)

gli è perchè pria di lordarla del tuo fetido sangue,
it is because before soiling it with your foul blood,

o svergognata, codesta lama, io vo' il suo nome! Parla!
oh shameless woman, this blade, I want his name! Speak!
(it is because I want his name before soiling my blade with your foul
blood, you shameless woman, I want his name! Speak!)

NEDDA
Vano è l'insulto. È muto il labbro mio.
Useless is the insult. Is mute the lip mine.
(Your insult is to no avail. My lips are sealed.)

CANIO
Il nome, non tardare, o donna!
The name, don't delay, oh woman!

NEDDA
No!

(Disegnato da parte argomentazione, Beppe appare nella parte
posteriore.)
(Drawn by the argument, Beppe appears at the back.)

No nol dirò giammai!
No, I won't say it, ever!

CANIO
(in una frenesia, correndo a Nedda)

(in a frenzy, rushing at Nedda)
Per la Madonna!
By the Madonna!
(By all that's holy!)

BEPPE
(frenare Canio e strappando il pugnale da lui)
(restraining Canio and snatching the dagger from him)
Padron! Che fate! Per l'amor di Dio!
Chief! What are you doing! For the love of God!

La gente esce di chiesa
The people are coming out of church

e a lo spettacolo qui muove!
and to the show here are moving!
(and are soon coming here to see the show!)

Andiamo, via, calmatevi!
Let's go, come, calm down!

CANIO
(cercando di liberarsi da Beppe)
(trying to free himself from Beppe)
Lasciami, Beppe! Il nome!
Let go, Beppe! The name!

BEPPE
(a Tonio)
(to Tonio)
Tonio, vieni a tenerlo.
Tonio, come to hold him.

CANIO
Il nome!

(Tonio prende Canio per un braccio e lo porta su un lato.)
(Tonio takes Canio by the arm and leads him to one side.)

Andiamo, arriva il pubblico! Vi spiegherete!
Let's go, is arriving the public! You'll settle it later!

(a Nedda)
(to Nedda)

E voi di lì tiratevi, andatevi a vestir.
And you from here get away, go to get dressed.

Sapete . . . Canio è violento, ma buon!
You know . . . Canio is hot-blooded but good-hearted!

CANIO
Infamia!
Disgrace!

(Beppe va in teatro con Nedda.)
(Beppe goes into the theater with Nedda.)

TONIO
(a Canio)
(to Canio)
Calmatevi, padrone . . . È meglio fingere;
Calm yourself, boss . . . It's better to pretend;

il ganzo tornerà. Di me fidatevi!
the pimp will return. In me trust!
                          (Trust me!)

Io la sorveglio. Ora facciam la recita.
I will watch her. Now let's do the show.

Chissà ch'egli non venga allo spettacolo e si tradisca!
Who knows that he might even come to the show and give himself
away!

Or via. Bisogna fingere per riuscir!
Now come. You need to pretend to succeed!

BEPPE
(di ritorno dal teatro)
(returning from the theater)
Andiamo, via, vestitevi, padrone.
Let's go, come, get dressed, boss.

E tu, batti la cassa, Tonio.
And you, beat the bass drum, Tonio.

(Beppe e Tonio si spengono dietro il teatro, lasciando solo Canio.)
(Beppe and Tonio go off behind the theater, leaving Canio alone.)

CANIO
Recitar! Mentre preso dal delirio
To perform! While seized by delirium
            (While in a state of frenzy)

non so più quel che dico e quel che faccio!
I don't know any longer what I am saying and what I'm doing!

Eppur è d'uopo sforzati! Bah! Sei tu forse un uom? . . .
Yet it must be done, force yourself! Bah! Are you maybe a man? . . .
                        (Are you not a man? . . .)

Tu sei Pagliaccio!
You are Pagliaccio!
(You're a clown!)

Vesti la giubba e la faccia infarina.
Put on your (clown's) smock and your face cover with flour.
                              (and put clown white on your face.)

La gente paga e rider vuole qua.
The people pay and laugh want here.
(The people pay and want to get their laughs.)

E se Arlecchin t'invola Colombina,
And if Arlecchin steals your Colombina,

ridi Pagliaccio, e ognun applaudirà!
laugh, Pagliaccio, and everyone will applaud!

Tramuta in lazzi lo spasmo ed il pianto;
Transmute into jest your heartbreak and the tears;

in una smorfia il singhiozzo e il dolor!
into a grimace your sob and your ache!
(and into a grimace your sob and your ache!)

Ah! Ridi, Pagliaccio, sul tuo amore infranto!
Ah! Laugh, clown, over your love shattered!

Ridi del duol che t'avvelena il cor!
Laugh at the pain that is poisoning your heart!

(Affranto e piangendo, Canio fa lentamente la strada per il teatro.)
(Heartbroken and weeping, Canio slowly makes his way to the theater.)

INTERMEZZO
INTERLUDE

ATTO SECONDO
ACT II

(La scena non cambia se non che è ormai tarda sera Beppe proviene da dietro il teatro, che suonava la tromba; Tonio lo segue battendo sul tamburo di ottone Beppe imposta le panchine per il pubblico. La gente arriva da tutte le parti.)

(The scene does not change except that it is now late evening. Beppe comes from behind the theater, blowing a trumpet; Tonio follows him, beating on the brass drum. Beppe sets up the benches for the public. People arrive from all sides.)

UOMINI E DONNE
MEN AND WOMEN
(variamente)
(variously)
Ohè! . . . Presto, affrettiamoci, svelto, compare . . .
Hey! . . . Quickly, let's hurry up, hurry, neighbor . . .

TONIO
Avanti!
Come here!

DONNE
WOMEN
. . . che lo spettacolo dee cominciare.
. . . for the show must begin.

UOMINI
MEN
O Dio! Che correre per giunger tosto!
Oh God! What rushing to arrive early!

TONIO
Si dà principio! Avanti!
We're starting! Come up!

UOMINI
MEN
Veh come corrono le bricconcelle!
Look how they're running, the rascal girls!

UOMINI, DONNE
MEN, WOMEN
Che correre, mio Dio . . .
What running, my God . . .

UOMINI
MEN
(per le donne)
(to the women)

Accomodatevi, comari belle!
Take your seat, ladies pretty!

(Silvio arriva e si siede accanto ad alcuni amici.)
(Silvio arrives and takes a seat next to some friends.)

TONIO
Pigliate posto!
Take your places!

PAESANI
VILLAGERS
Cerchiamo posto! Cerchiam di metterci ben sul davanti!
We're looking for a place! Let's try to get comfortably in front!

Che lo spettacolo dee cominciare.

Via, su spicciatervi! Perchè tardate mai? Siam tutti là!
Come on, hurry! Why delay so? We're all here!

(Tonio va al retro del teatro, portando il tamburo. Beppe viene in aiuto alcune donne litigiosi per trovare posti a sedere.)
(Tonio goes to the back of the theater, carrying the drum. Beppe comes to help some squabbling women to find places to sit.)

DONNE
WOMEN
Ma non pigiatevi! Fa caldo! Su, Beppe, aiutaci . . .
But don't squash! It's hot! Come, Beppe, help us . . .

V'è posto accanto!
There's room besides us!

UOMINI
MEN
Veh! S'accapigliano! Chiamano aiuto!
Look! They're seizing each other by the hair! They are calling for help!

Sedetevi, via, senza gridar!
Sit down, come, without shouting!

BEPPE
Sedetevi, via, senza gridar!

(Silvo ha avvicinato Nedda, che sta andando in giro a raccogliere i soldi.)
(Silvo has approached Nedda, who is going around collecting money.)

SILVIO
Nedda!

NEDDA
Sii cauto! Non t'ha veduto!
Be careful! He hasn't seen you!

SILVIO
Verrò ad attenderti. Non obliar!
I'll be waiting for you. Don't forget!

(Nedda continua a raccogliere denaro.)
(Nedda continues to collect money.)

UOMINI E DONNE
MEN AND WOMEN
Suvvia, spicciatevi! Perchè tardate? Orsù! Incominciate! Perchè indugiate?
Come on, hurry up! Why delay? Come! Start! What's the holdup?

BEPPE
Che furia! Diavolo! Prima pagate. Nedda, incassate!
What frenzy! The devil! First pay up. Nedda, take the money!

UOMINI E DONNE
MEN AND WOMEN
Di qua! Di qua!
Here . . . there!

Perchè tardar? Spicciate, incominciate!

Suvvia questa commedia! Facciam rumore!
On with this comedy! Let's make noise!

Diggià suonar ventitré ore!
Already sounded seven o'clock!

Allo spettacolo ognun anela!
For the show everyone longs!
(Everyone is dying to see the show!)

(Una campana si sente all'interno del teatro. Ci sono grida di soddisfazione dal pubblico.)
(A bell is heard inside the theater. There are shouts of satisfaction from the public.)

UOMINI
MEN
S'alza la tela!
It's going up, the curtain!

Silenzio! Olà!
Silence! Ho there!

IL GIOCO
THE PLAY

Nedda *(Colombina)*—Beppe *(Arlecchino)*
Canio *(Pagliaccio)*—Tonio *(Taddeo)*

(Le tende nel piccolo teatro all'aperto. Il set di circa dipinto mostra una piccola rom con due porte sul lato e una sala praticabili sul retro. C'è un tavolo e due sedie rustiche. Nedda, vestita da Colombina, è seduto vicino al tavolo guardando con impazienza di volta in volta verso la porta. Dopo un po 'si alza, va alla finestra e guarda fuori, poi ritorna tot ha piedi del Stagge, dove si cammina avanti e indietro senza sosta.)

(The curtains in the little theater open. The roughly painted set shows a small room with two doors on the side and a practicable room at the back. There is a table and two rustic chairs. Nedda, dressed as Colombina, is seated near the table, looking impatiently from time to time towards the door. After a bit she gets up, goes to the window and looks out, then returns to the foot of the stage, where she paces back and forth restlessly.)

COLOMBINA (NEDDA)
Pagliaccio, mio marito, a tarda notte sol tornerà.
Pagliaccio, my husband, at late night only will return.
(will return only late at night.)

E quello scimunito di Taddeo perchè mai non è ancor qua?
And that oaf of a Taddeo why then isn't he yet here?

(Sente pizzicato di chitarra fuori, lei emette un grido di gioia e corre alla finestra.)
(She hears the pizzicato of a guitar outside; she utters a cry of joy and runs to the window.)

ARLECCHINO (BEPPE)
Oh Colombina, il tenero fido Arlecchin è a te vicin!
Oh Colombina, the tender true Arlecchin is to you near!

Di te chiamando e sospirando aspetta il poverin!
For you calling and sighing awaits the poor thing!

La tua faccetta mostrami, ch'io vo' baciar, senza tardar
Your little face show me, that I want to kiss, without delay

la tua boccuccia. Amor mi cruccia, e mi sta a tormentar!
your little mouth. Love tortures me, and is tormenting me!

Oh Colombina schiudimi il finestrin,

Oh Colombina open to me the little window,

che a te vicin, di te chiamando e sospirando
who to you is near, for you calling and sighing

è il povero Arlecchin!
is (the) poor Arlecchin!

COLOMBINA (NEDDA)
(scendendo fase)
(coming down stage)
Di fare il segno convenuto appressa l'istante,
To give the signal agreed upon nears the moment,
(The moment is nearing for me to give him the agreed upon signal,)

ed Arlecchino aspetta!
and Arlecchino is waiting!

(Nedda si siede al tavolo, volgendo le spalle alla porta. Entra Tonio vestito come il servo Taddeo, non visto da Nedda, e si arresta a contemplarla.)
(She sits at the table again. Taddeo opens the door and stops to gaze at Colombina. He has a basket in his hand.)

TADDEO (TONIO)
È dessa!
It's she!

(comicamente alzando le mani e cesto verso il cielo)
(comically raising his hands and basket towards heaven)

Dei, com'è bella!
Gods, how she is beautiful!

(Il pubblico ride.)
(The audience laughs.)

Se alla rubella io disvelassi
If to that scornful girl I revealed

l'amor mio che commuove fino i sassi!
my love which moves to pity even the stones!

Lungi è lo sposo, perchè non oso?
Far away is her husband, why don't I dare?

Soli noi siamo e senza alcun sospetto!
Alone we are and without any suspicion!
(We are alone and no one suspects a thing!)

Orsù. Proviamo!
Come now. Let me try!

(Sospiro lungo, esagerato. Il pubblico ride.)
(He utters a loud and exaggerated sigh. The public laughs.)

COLOMBINA (NEDDA)
(rivolgendosi a lui senza aumento)
(turning to him without rising)
Sei tu, bestia?
Is it you, beast?[3]

TADDEO (TONIO)
(in piedi molto ancora)
(standing very still)
Quell'io sono, sì!
He I am, yes!

COLOMBINA (NEDDA)
E Pagliaccio è partito?
And Pagliaccio, has he left?

TADDEO (TONIO)
Egli partì!
He left!

(Fischia. Le risate pubblici.)
(He whistles. The public laughs.)

COLOMBINA (NEDDA)
Che fai così impalato? Il pollo hai tu comprato?
What are you doing so bold upright? The chicken, have you bought it?

TADDEO (TONIO)
Ecco, vergin divina!
Here it is, maiden divine!

(Si alza in ginocchio, offrendo il cestello.)
(He gets on his knees, offering the basket.)

Ed anzi, eccoci entrambi ai piedi tuoi!
And moreover, here we are both of us, at the feet yours!
(And moreover, here we are, the chicken and I, at your feet!)

Poichè l'ora è suonata, O Colombina,
Since the hour has sounded, oh Colombina,

di svelarti il mio cor.
to bare you my heart.
(to bare my soul to you.)

Di', udirmi vuoi?
Say, hear me do you wish?
(Say, will you hear me out?)

Dal dì . . .
From the day . . .

COLOMBINA (NEDDA)
(interrompendo)
(interrupting)

Quanto spendesti dal trattore?
How much did you spend at the innkeeper?

TADDEO (TONIO)
Uno e cinquanta.
One fifty.

Da quel dì il mio core . . .
From that day my heart . . .

COLOMBINA (NEDDA)
Non seccarmi, Taddeo!
Don't annoy me, Taddeo!

TADDEO (TONIO)
(con intento maligno)
(with snide intention)
So che sei pura e casta al par di neve!
I know that you're pure and chaste like snow!

(Arlecchino scavalca la finestra, e mette sul tavolo una bottiglia; poi va verso Taddeo mentre questo finge di non vederlo.)

*(Meanwhile Arlecchino enters through the window, puts downt he bottle of
wine he is carrying and creeps stealthily behind Taddeo.)*

E ben che dura ti mostri, dura,
And although hard you show yourself to be, hard,

ad obbliarti io non riesco!
to forget you I cannot bring myself!
(I can never bring myself to forget you!)

ARLECCHINO (BEPPE)
*(prendendo Taddeo da un orecchio e dandogli un calcio sul suo
didietro)*
(taking Taddeo by an ear and giving him a kick on his backside)
Va a pigliar fresco!
Go get (some) fresh air!

(Risate.)
(Laughter.)

TADDEO (TONIO)
Numi! S'aman! M'arrendo ai detti tuoi!
Ye Gods! They're in love! I yield to the words yours!
                              (I'll do whatever you say!)

(Lui allarga le braccia in un gesto solenne benedizione comico.)
(He extends his arms in a solemn comical benediction gesture.)

Vi benedico!
I bless you!

(andando indietro verso l'ingresso)
(going back towards the entrance)

Là veglio su voi!
There I will watch over you!

(Ha lasciato. Le risate pubblici. Colombina e Arlecchino guardano l'un l'altro con affetto esagerato.)

(He leaves. The public laughs. Colombina and Arlecchino look at one another with exaggerated affection.)

COLOMBINA (NEDDA)
Arlecchin!

ARLECCHINO (BEPPE)
Colombina! Alfin s'arrenda ai nostri prieghi amor!
Colombina! At last let it yield to our prayers love!
(Let love at last yield to our prayers!)

(Si abbracciano l'un l'altro comicamente.)
(They embrace one another comically.)

COLOMBINA (NEDDA)
Facciam merenda.
Let's have supper.

(Colombina imposta il tavolo per due e mette il pollo in tavola. Arlecchino va a prendere la bottiglia di vino che aveva portato con sé mentre entrava.)
(Colombina sets the table for two and puts the chicken on the table. Arlecchino goes to get the bottle of wine he had brought with him as he entered.)

Guarda, amor mio, che splendida cenetta preparai!
Look, my love, what splendid little supper I've prepared!

ARLECCHINO (BEPPE)
Guarda, amor mio, che nettare divino t'apportai!
Look, my love, what nectar divine I brought you!

COLOMBINA, ARLECCHINO (NEDDA, BEPPE)
(seduto al tavolo)
(sitting at the table)
Ah! L'amor ama gli effluvi del vin, de la cucina!
Ah! Love loves the smell of wine, of cooking!

ARLECCHINO (BEPPE)
Mia ghiotta Colombina!
My gluttonous Colombina!

COLOMBINA (NEDDA)
Amabile beone!
Adorable tippler!

ARLECCHINO (BEPPE)
(prendendo un'ampolletta)
(taking out a phial from his tunic)
Prendi questo narcotico; dallo a Pagliaccio
Take this narcotic; give it to Pagliaccio

pria che s'addormenti e poi fuggiam insiem!
before he goes to sleep and then let's run away together!

COLOMBINA (NEDDA)
Sì, porgi!
Yes, give it here!

TADDEO (TONIO)
(entrando, fingendo timore e tremore)
(entering, feigning fear and trembling)

Attenti! Pagliaccio è là tutto stravolto!
Beware! Pagliaccio is here, all a-raging!

Ed armi cerca! Io corro a barricarmi!
And weapons he searches for! I'll run for cover!

(Egli lascia.)
(He leaves.)

COLOMBINA (NEDDA)
(ad Arlecchino)
(to Arlecchino)
Via!
Off you go!

(Arlecchino arrampica fuori dalla finestra.)
(Arlecchino climbs out the window.)

ARLECCHINO (BEPPE)
(scavalca la finestra)
(reappearing at the window)
Versa il filtro nella tazza sua!
Pour the philter in the cup his!
(Pour the sleeping potion into his cup!)

(Scompare.)
(He disappears.)

COLOMBINA (NEDDA)
(alla finestra)
(at the window)
A stanotte . . . e per sempre tua.
Till tonight . . . and forever yours.

(Canio, in costume da clown, passa attraverso la porta e sente le ultime parole di Nedda.)
(Canio, in clown costume, comes through the door and hears Nedda's last words.)

PAGLIACCIO (CANIO)
Nome di Dio, le stesse parole!
Name of God, the same words!

(Venendo ora a svolgere il suo ruolo di Pagliaccio.)
(Coming forward to play his role as Pagliaccio.)

Coraggio!
Courage!

(Alta voce, giocando Pagliaccio.)
(Aloud, playing Pagliaccio.)

Un uomo era con te!
A man was with you!

COLOMBINA (NEDDA)
Che fole! Sei briaco?
What nonsense! Are you drunk?

PAGLIACCIO (CANIO)
(a malapena in grado di controllare se stesso)
(barely able to control himself)
Briaco! Sì . . . da un'ora!
Drunk! Yes . . . since an hour (ago)!

COLOMBINA (NEDDA)
Tornasti presto.
You came back early.

PAGLIACCIO (CANIO)
Ma in tempo! T'accora! Dolce sposina!
But in time! Does it distress you! Sweet little wife!

(Cercando di controllarsi.)
(Trying to control himself.)

Ah! Sola io ti credea e due posti son là!
Ah! Alone I believed you to be and two places are there!
(I thought you were alone, but you set two places at the table there!)

COLOMBINA (NEDDA)
Con me sedea Taddeo,
With me was sitting Taddeo,

che là si chiuse per paura!
who over there locked himself in out of fear!

Orsù . . . parla!
Come . . . speak up!

TADDEO (TONIO)
(con un ghigno nella sua voce, fingendo paura)
(with a sneer in his voice, feigning fear)
Credetela! Essa è pura!!
Believe her! She is pure!!

E aborre dal mentir quel labbro pio!!
And hates to lie that lip pious!!
(And those pious lips hate to lie!!)

(Risate.)
(Laughter.)

CANIO
(in una furia)
(in a fury)
Per la morte! Smettiamo!
By death! Enough!
(Death and damnation!)

Ho dritto anch'io d'agir come ogni altr'uomo! Il nome suo . . .
I have the right also I to act like any other man! His name . . .

COLOMBINA (NEDDA)
Di chi?
Of who?
(Whose name?)

CANIO
Vo' il nome dell'amante tuo,
I want the name of your lover,

del drudo infame a cui ti desti in braccio,
of the lover damned to whom you gave yourself in the arms,
(of that damned lover in whose arms you threw yourself,)

O turpe donna!
oh filthy woman!

COLOMBINA (NEDDA)
(sempre recitando la commedia)
(trying to recall him to his part)
Pagliaccio! Pagliaccio!

CANIO
No, Pagliaccio non son. Se il viso è pallido
No, Pagliaccio I am not. If my face is pale

è di vergogna e smania di vendetta!
it's out of shame and frenzy for revenge!

L'uom riprende i suoi dritti, e 'l cor che sanguina
A man reassumes his rights, and his heart that bleeds

vuol sangue a lavar l'onta, O maledetta!
wants blood to wash away the shame, oh cursed woman!

No, Pagliaccio non son,

son quei che stolido ti raccolse orfanella in su la via
I'm the one who foolishly picked you up, an orphan, on the street

quasi morta di fame e un nome offriati,
almost dead from hunger and a name I gave you,

ed un amor ch'era febbre e follia!
and a love that was fever and folly!

DONNE
WOMEN
Comare, mi fa piangere! Par vera questa scena!
Neighbor, it makes me weep! It seems true this scene!

UOMINI
MEN
Zitte laggiù! . . . Che diamine![4]
Quiet down there! . . . What the devil!

SILVIO
(a parte)
(aside)
Io mi ritengo appena!

I restrain myself hardly!

CANIO
Sperai, tanto il delirio accecato m'avea
I hoped, so much my passion blinded had me

se non amor, pietà . . . mercè!
if not love (at least) pity . . . mercy!
(I had hoped, so blinded by passion was I, if not love from you, at least some pity or mercy!)

Ed ogni sacrifizio al cor, lieto imponeva,
And every sacrifice on my heart happily I imposed,

e fidente credea più che in Dio stesso, in te!
and trustingly I believed more than in God himself, in you!
(and trustingly believed in you more than in God himself!)

Ma il vizio alberga sol nell'alma tua negletta;
But (the) vice has place only in the soul yours neglected;
(But only vice has place in your neglected soul;)

sol legge è il senso a te!
only law is sensuality to you!
(the only law you know is sensuality!)

Va, non merti il mio duol, O meretrice abbietta!
Go, you don't deserve my tears, oh harlot abject!
                                        (you abject harlot!)

Vo' nello sprezzo mio scacciarti sotto i piè!
I want in the disgust mine crush you under my feet!

UOMINI E DONNE
MEN AND WOMEN
Bravo!

NEDDA
Ebben, se mi giudichi di te indegna,
Well then, if you think me of you unworthy,

mi scaccia in questo istante . . .
throw me out in this moment . . .

CANIO
(sogghignando)
(laughing)
Ah! Ah! Di meglio chiedere non dei
Ha ha! A better thing ask you shouldn't

che correr già al tuo caro amante. Sei furba!
than to run right away to your dear lover. You're clever!
(You'd like nothing better than to run to your dear lover right
away. You're clever!)

No! Per Dio! Tu resterai,
No! By God! You will stay,

e 'l nome del tuo ganzo mi dirai!!
and the name of your pimp you will tell me!!

NEDDA
(cercando di riprendere la commedia)
(trying to get back to the comedy script, smiling)
Suvvia, così terribile davver non ti credeo!
Come on, so terrible in truth not I believed you to be!
(Come on, I would have never thought you were such an ogre!)

Qui nulla v'ha di tragico.
Here nothing there is that's tragic.
(There's nothing here that's so serious.)

Vieni a dirgli, O Taddeo,
Come to tell him, oh Taddeo,

che l'uom seduto or dianzi a me vicino era
that the man seated just now to me close was

il pauroso ed innocuo Arlecchino!
the fearful and innocuous Arlecchino!
(tell him that the man who just now was seated close to me was none
other than the frightened and innocuous Arlecchino!)

(Risate, che viene interrotta dalla espressione di Canio.)
(Laughter, which is cut short by Canio's expression.)

CANIO
Ah! Tu mi sfidi! E ancor non l'hai capita ch'io non ti cedo?
Ah! You defy me! And still have not understood that I won't let you go?

Il nome, o la tua vita!
His name, or your life!

NEDDA
No, per mia madre!
No, by my mother!

Indegna esser poss'io quello che vuoi,
Unworthy to be can I as much as you say,

ma vile non son, per Dio!
but a coward I am not, by God!

PAESANI
VILLAGERS
(variamente)
(variously)
Fanno davvero? . . . Seria è la cosa e scura!
Are they in earnest? . . . Serious is the matter and grim!

Zitti laggiù!
Hush down there!

SILVIO
Io non resisto più! Oh, la strana commedia!
I can't stand it any longer! Oh, the strange play!

(Beppe appare nella parte posteriore, trattenuta da Tonio.)
(Beppe appears at the back, held back by Tonio.)

BEPPE
Bisogna uscire, Tonio.
We must leave, Tonio.

TONIO
(ancora in mano a lui)
(still holding on to him)
Taci, sciocco!
Quiet, fool!

NEDDA
Di quel tuo sdegno è l'amor mio più forte!
Of your anger is my love stronger!

BEPPE
Ho paura!
I'm afraid!

CANIO
Ah!

NEDDA
Non parlerò! No! A costo della morte!
I won't talk! No! Even at cost of my death!

CANIO
Il nome!

NEDDA
No!

(C'è una confusione generale tra il pubblico. Ognuno si alza in piedi.)
(There is a general confusion among the public. Everyone rises to their feet.)

SILVIO
Santo diavolo! Fa davvero!
Holy devil! He's in earnest!

(Alcuni abitanti del villaggio trattenere Silvio, ignaro del motivo della sua furia. Alcune donne si precipitano fuori, spaventato. Nedda corre verso il pubblico per la protezione, ma Canio lei afferra e la trafigge con un coltello.)
(Some villagers hold back Silvio, unaware of the reason for his fury. Some women rush out, frightened. Nedda runs towards the audience for protection, but Canio seizes her and stabs her with a knife.)

BEPPE, PAESANI
BEPPE, VILLAGERS
Che fai!
What are you doing!

CANIO
(gettando il coltello in Nedda)
(plunging his knife into Nedda)
A te!
Take that!

(Nedda cade, ferito a morte.)
(Nedda falls, mortally wounded.)

BEPPE, PAESANI
BEPPE, VILLAGERS
Ferma!
Stop!

CANIO
Di morte negli spasimi lo dirai!
Of death in the throes you will tell me!

NEDDA
(con uno sforzo supremo)
(with a supreme effort)
Soccorso! Silvio!
Help! Silvio!

SILVIO
Nedda!

CANIO
Ah! Sei tu? Ben venga!
Ah! Is it you? Welcome!

(Canio si precipita a Silvio e affonda il coltello nel suo cuore.)
(Canio rushes to Silvio and plunges his knife into his heart.)

SILVIO
(che cade come se colpito da un fulmine)
(falling as if struck by lightning)
Ah!

DONNE
WOMEN
Gesummaria!
Jesus Mary!

UOMINI
MEN
Arresta!
Stop!

CANIO
(al pubblico)
(to the public)
La commedia è finita!
The comedy is over!

(Come se stupefatto, Canio cade il coltello.)
(As if stupefied, Canio drops his knife.)

FINE DELL'OPERA
END OF THE OPERA

NOTES

Nico Castel

Cavalleria Rusticana

1. This *Siciliana* is customarily sung in the Sicilian dialect, even though an Italian version is shown in some scores, as follows: **O Lola bianca come fior di spino, quando t'affaci te, s'affaccia il sole; chi t'ha baciato il labbro porporino grazia più bella a Dio chieder non vôle. C'è scritto sangue sopra la tua porta, ma di restarci a me non me n'importa; se per te mojo e vado in paradiso, non c'entro se non vedo il tuo bel viso.** The meaning is practically the same.

2. Notice that in the Sicilian language in words like *cirasa, cammisa, vasu, risa, accisu, paradisu,* and *trasu,* the inter-vocalic *s* is being transcribed as an [s] sound and not a [z]. This is a left-over *Spanishism*, from centuries ago when the Spanish crown occupied the territory of Sicily.

3. This is a weaver's instrument for passing a thread of the woof from one side of the cloth to the other between the threads of the warp.

4. *Santuzza* is a Sicilian diminutive for the name *Santa*. In Turiddu's "Addio alla mamma" later on, he calls her *Santa*.

5. *Turiddu* is a Sicilian diminutive for *Salvatore*.

6. Affairs out of wedlock at this time and in such a strict small Catholic village would certainly cause a young woman to be excommunicated by the church. In all probability, even though it is never mentioned in the opera, Santuzza is with child, an even greater reason for excommunication.

7. In this section Mascagni has put strong musical offbeats on the usually unstressed syllables of *Lola* and *consola*. The phonetics reflect the shifted stress.

8. Notice the subtle change of verbal mood from *scalpita* and *squillano* to *scalpiti* and *squillino*. In the first verse it is "the horse paws the ground and the bells jingle"; in the repeat it is "let the horse paw the ground and the bells jingle."

9. It is important, especially in this highly charged emotional encounter, that the singer observe the *raddoppiamenti* as shown in the phonetics: *Assai più bbella è Llola*. The name *Lola* has to drip with hate, and needs the double *l* for emphasis. Likewise, Lola's beauty has to be referred to sarcastically with a strong *raddoppiamento*.

10. There is a subtle double meaning in this phrase with the word *lui*, which may also mean "there isn't in heaven an angel as handsome as Turiddu."

11. *Tetta* means "roof," but in poetry it also means "house" or "home." The "decorations" she is referring to are the horns of the cuckold. The use of the word *tetto* in this case may also be a reference to Alfio's head, where the horns are "decorating" it.

12. *Ferro* really means "iron," but in poetry it also means "a dagger, a knife, a sword, or any type of blade weapon."

Pagliacci

1. Many assume that this refers to the twenty-four-hour clock designation used in the army and in many European countries, or "twenty-three-hundred-hours," which in a normal situation would be 11:00 p.m. My esteemed colleague, conductor

Joseph Colaneri, has come up with a clarification on this matter, and it gives me pleasure to quote his comment:

> In the opera the townspeople depart for Vespers after Canio's final *a ventitre ore*, the time given for the start of the *commedia*. Vespers would have taken place just before sunset. The people sing "*Din, don, diggià i culmini il sol vuol baciar*" ("already the sun is kissing the mountain tops"—i.e., it is setting). After Canio and Nedda have their confrontation, Beppe exhorts Canio to get dressed for the performance since the townspeople are now leaving the church and are arriving directly for the performance. (*La gente esce di chiesa e a lo spettocolo qui muove*). If sunset would occur in Italy during *Mezz'agosto* (as Nedda says in her *Ballatella*) at approximately 8:00 p.m., the townspeople would be arriving for the *commedia* sometime before that.

It is also a fact that in certain parts of 19th-century Italy, the first "hour" was calculated as beginning with the *angelus* bell, rung at dusk. The twenty-third hour would then occur an hour before dusk, around 7:00 p.m.

2. *Vanno* really means "they go." However, since we are talking about birds, I have chosen to use "fly."

3. *Bestia*, in addition to "beast," also can be employed to call someone "fool."

4. Devil is actually *diavolo*. *Diamine* is really a milder euphemism combining letters of <u>*dia*</u>*volo* and <u>*do*</u>*mine* (the Lord).